EASY GUITAR
WITH NOTES & TAB

TOP WORSHIP HITS

ISBN 978-1-61780-555-4

HAL•LEONARD®
CORPORATION

7777 W. BLUEMOUND RD. P.O. BOX 13819 MILWAUKEE, WI 53213

Visit Hal Leonard Online at
www.halleonard.com

CONTENTS

STRUM AND PICK PATTERNS

This chart contains the suggested strum and pick patterns that are referred to by number at the beginning
of each song in this book. The symbols ⊓ and ∨ in the strum patterns refer to down and up strokes, respectively.
The letters in the pick patterns indicate which right-hand fingers play which strings.

p = thumb
i = index finger
m = middle finger
a = ring finger

For example; Pick Pattern 2
is played: thumb - index - middle - ring

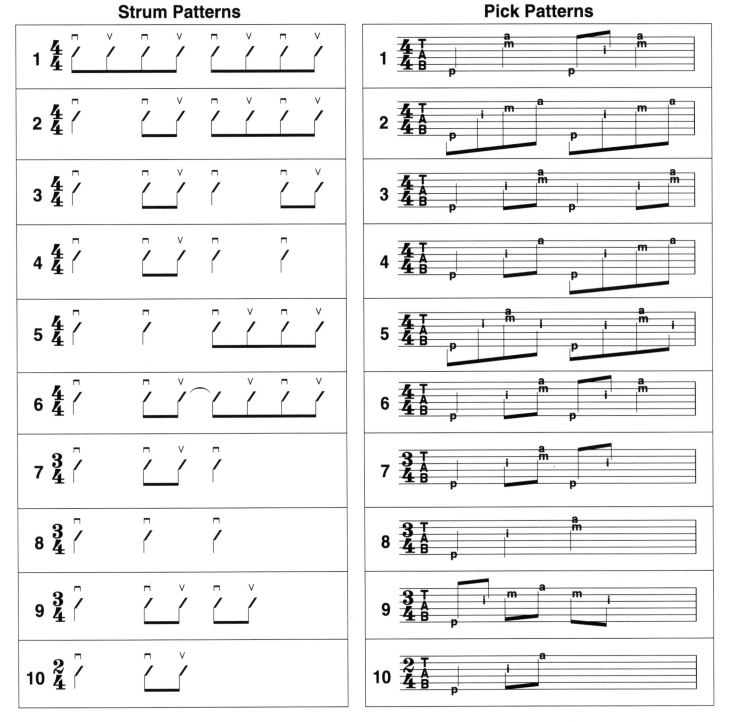

You can use the 3/4 Strum and Pick Patterns in songs written in compound meter (6/8, 9/8, 12/8, etc.).
For example, you can accompany a song in 6/8 by playing the 3/4 pattern twice in each measure.
The 4/4 Strum and Pick Patterns can be used for songs written in cut time (¢) by doubling the note
time values in the patterns. Each pattern would therefore last two measures in cut time.

Came to My Rescue

Words and Music by Marty Sampson, Dylan Thomas and Joel Davies

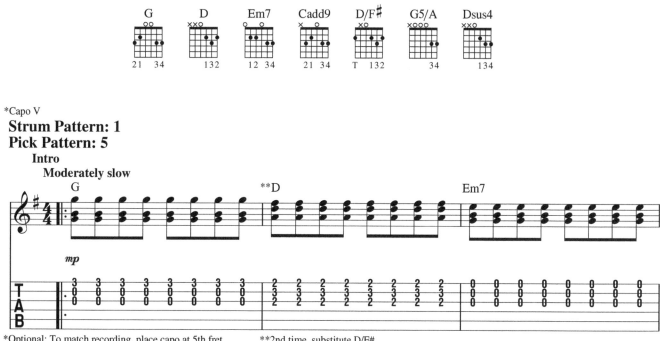

*Capo V

Strum Pattern: 1
Pick Pattern: 5

Intro
Moderately slow

*Optional: To match recording, place capo at 5th fret.   **2nd time, substitute D/F#

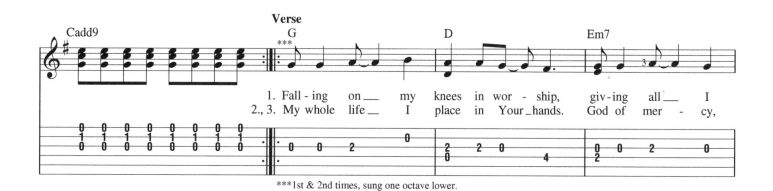

Verse

1. Fall - ing on __ my knees in wor - ship, giv-ing all __ I
2., 3. My whole life __ I place in Your __ hands. God of mer - cy,

***1st & 2nd times, sung one octave lower.

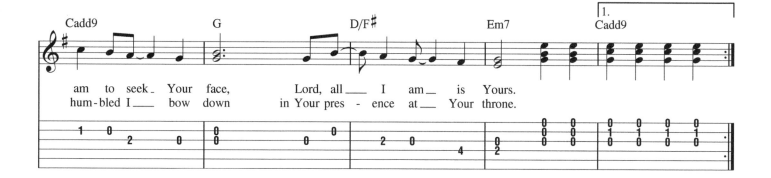

am to seek __ Your face, Lord, all __ I am __ is Yours.
hum-bled I __ bow down in Your pres - ence at __ Your throne.

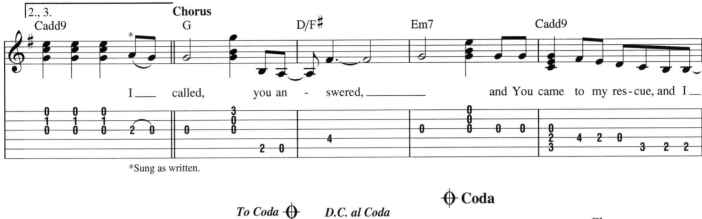

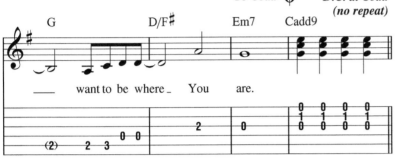

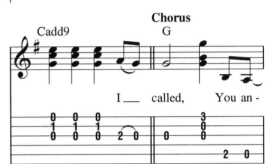

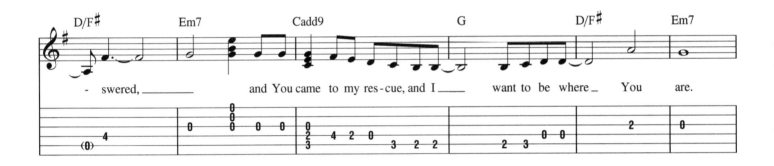

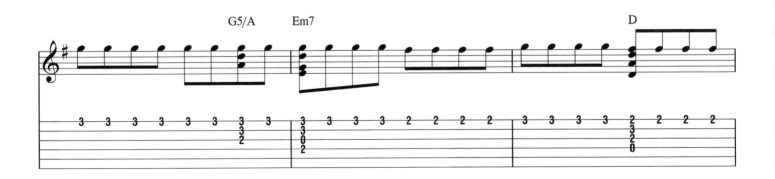

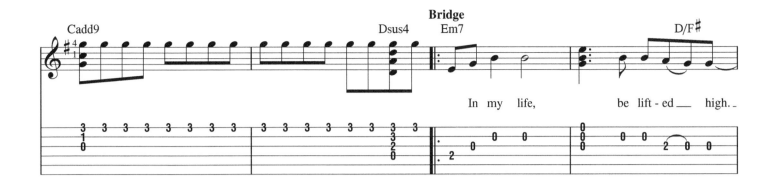

In my life, be lift-ed ___ high. ___

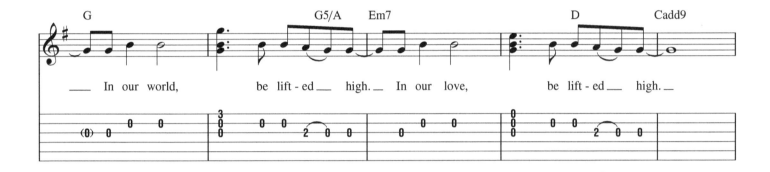

In our world, be lift-ed ___ high. ___ In our love, be lift-ed ___ high. ___

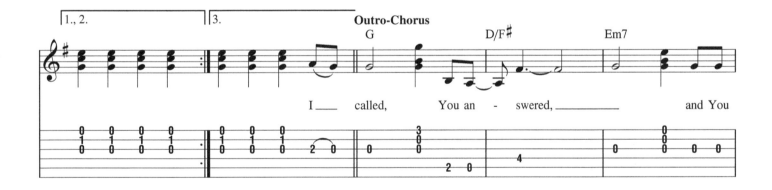

I ___ called, You an - swered, _____ and You

came to my res-cue, and I _____ want to be where ___ You are.

Awesome Is the Lord Most High

Words and Music by Chris Tomlin, Jesse Reeves, Cary Pierce and Jon Abel

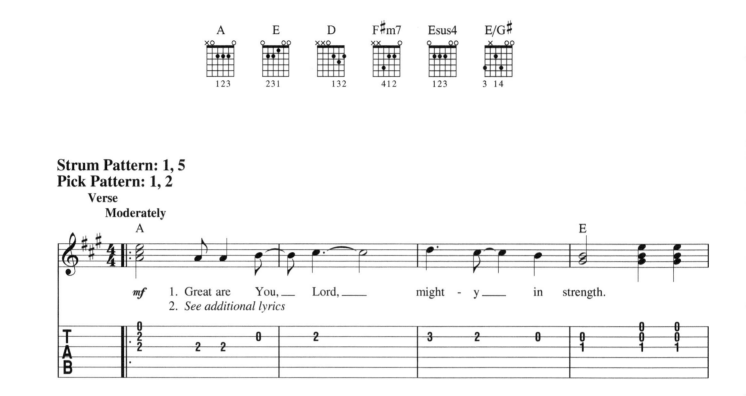

Strum Pattern: 1, 5
Pick Pattern: 1, 2

Verse
Moderately

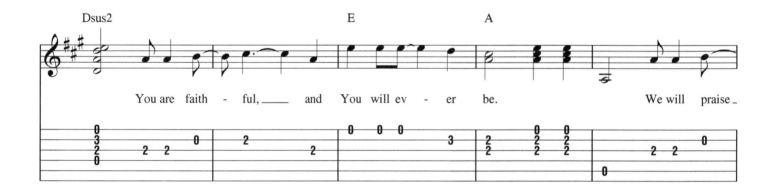

1. Great are You,___ Lord,___ might - y___ in strength.
2. *See additional lyrics*

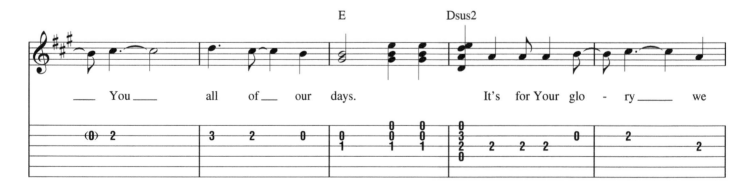

You are faith - ful,___ and You will ev - er be.   We will praise___

___ You ___ all of ___ our days.   It's for Your glo - ry ___ we

of - fer ev - 'ry - thing. Raise your hands all you na - tions, shout to God all cre - a -

- tion, ___ how awe - some _ is the Lord most high. We will

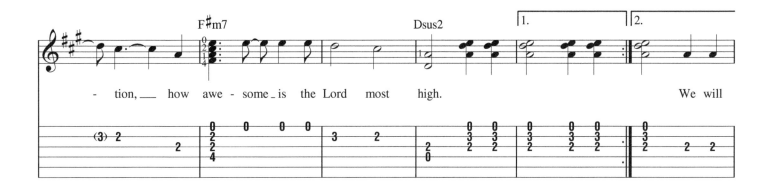

praise You to-geth - er, ___ for now and for-ev - er. ___ How awe - some _ is the

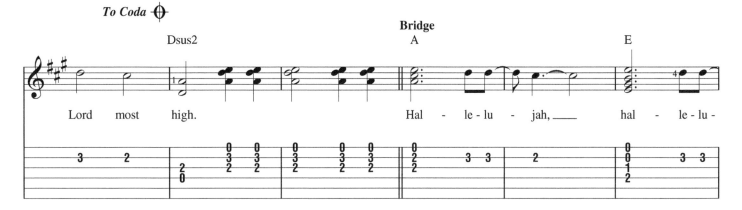

Lord most high. Hal - le - lu - jah, ___ hal - le - lu -

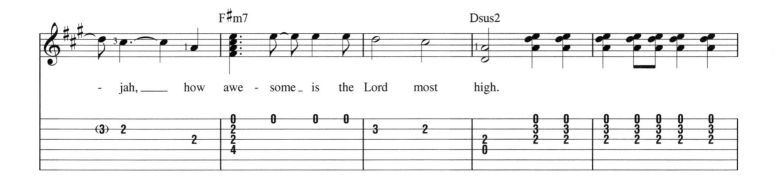

- jah, ___ how awe - some _ is the Lord most high.

Hal - le - lu - jah, ___ hal - le - lu - jah, ___ how awe - some _ is the Lord most

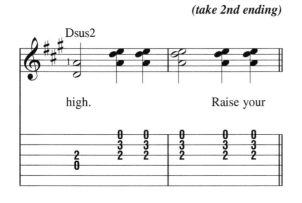

D.S. al Coda
(take 2nd ending)

high. Raise your

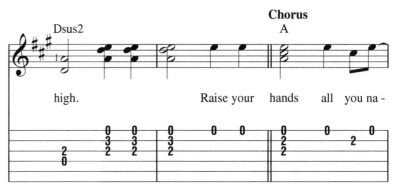

 Coda

Chorus

high. Raise your hands all you na -

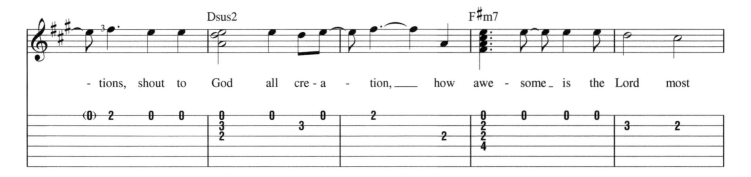

- tions, shout to God all cre - a - tion, ___ how awe - some _ is the Lord most

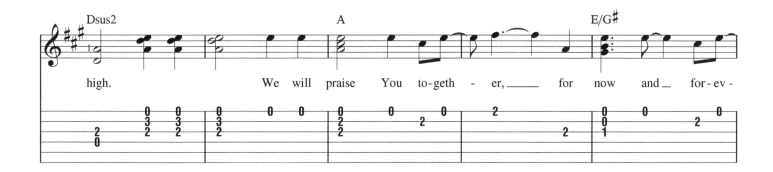

high. We will praise You to-geth - er, _____ for now and _ for - ev -

- er. _____ How awe - some _ is the Lord most high, the Lord most _ high.

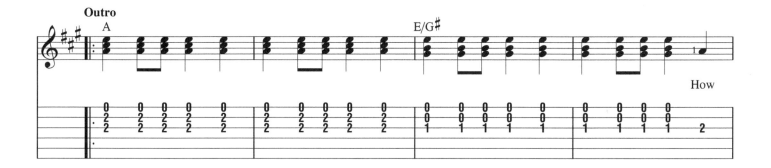

Outro

How

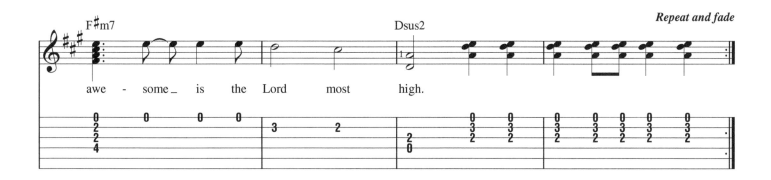

Repeat and fade

awe - some _ is the Lord most high.

Additional Lyrics

2. Where You send us, God we will go.
   You're the answer, we want the world to know.
   We will trust You when You call our name.
   Where You lead us, we'll follow all the way.

Beautiful One

Words and Music by Tim Hughes

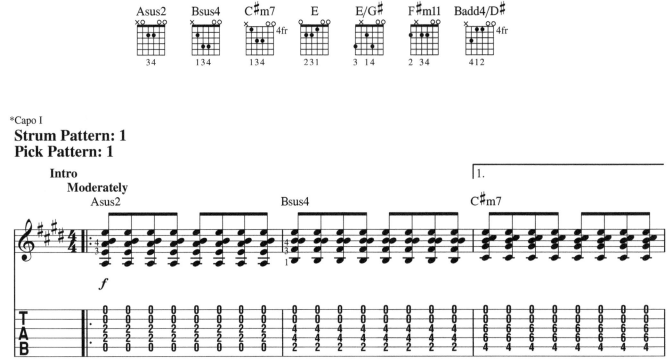

*Capo I

Strum Pattern: 1
Pick Pattern: 1

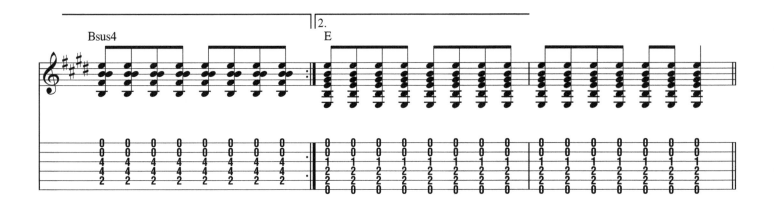

*Optional: To match recording, place capo at 1st fret.

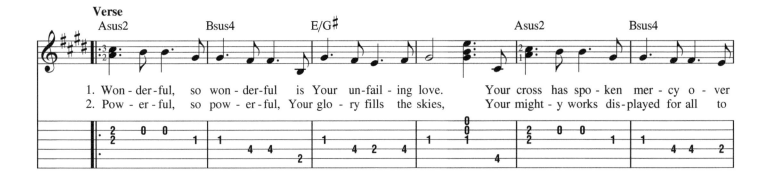

1. Won - der - ful,   so won - der - ful   is Your un - fail - ing love.   Your cross has spo - ken mer - cy o - ver
2. Pow - er - ful,   so pow - er - ful, Your glo - ry fills   the skies,   Your might - y works dis - played for all   to

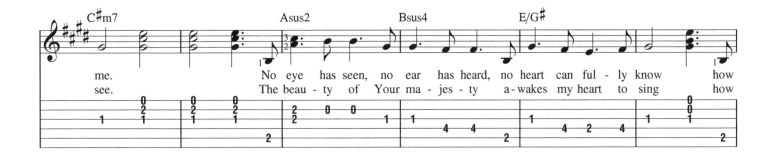

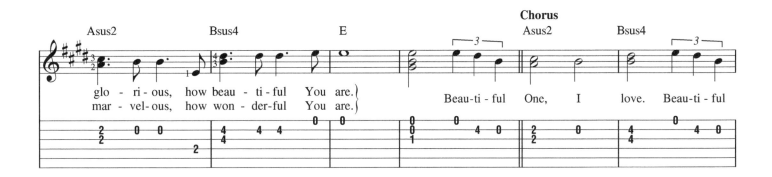

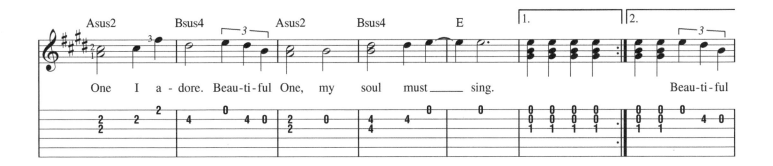

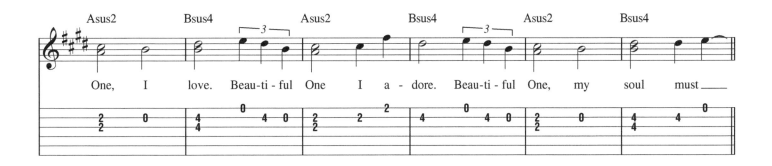

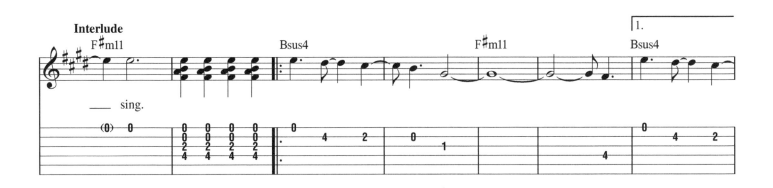

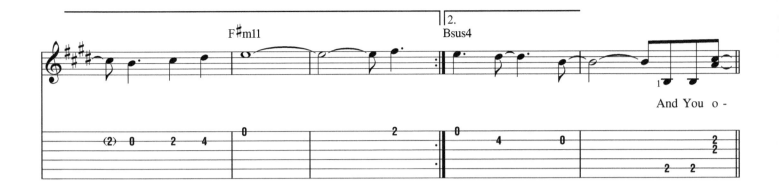

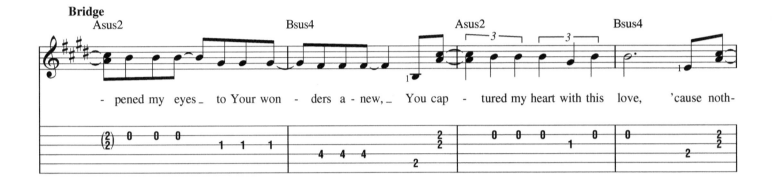

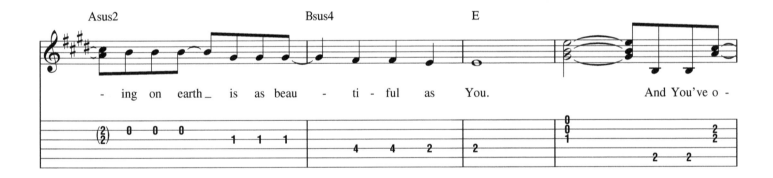

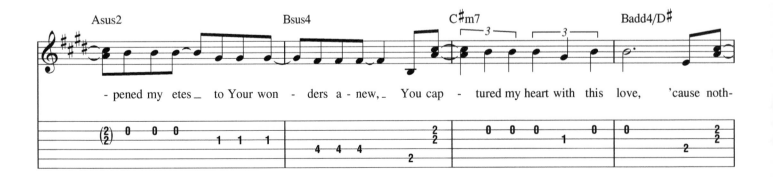

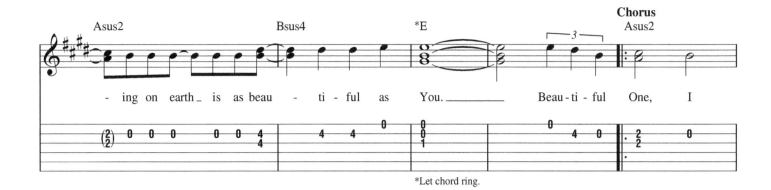

*Let chord ring.

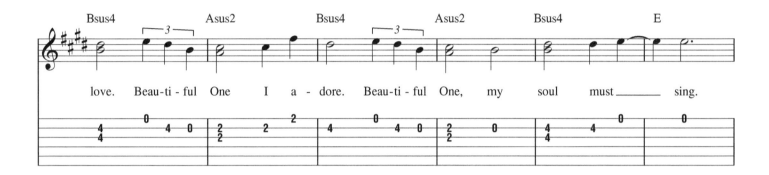

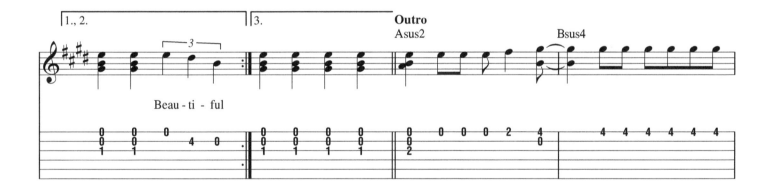

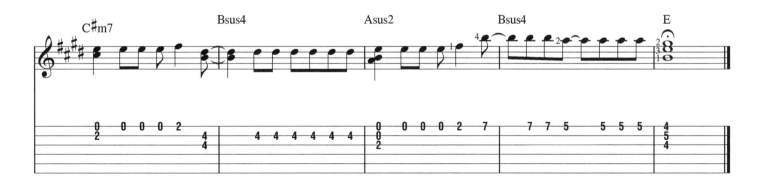

Blessed Be Your Name

Words and Music by Matt Redman and Beth Redman

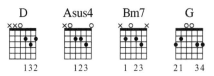

*Tune down 1/2 step:
(low to high) Eb-Ab-Db-Gb-Bb-Eb

Strum Pattern: 1
Pick Pattern: 3

Intro
Moderately

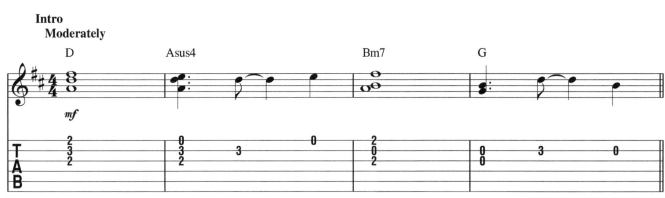

*Optional: To match recording, tune down 1/2 step.

Verse

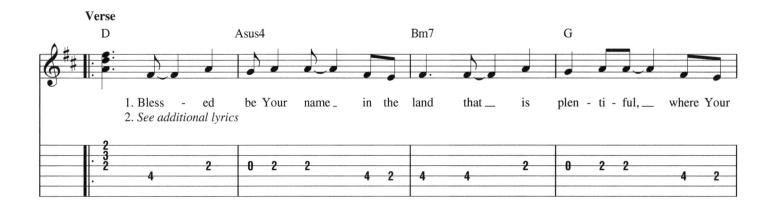

1. Bless - ed   be Your   name __ in the   land   that __ is   plen - ti - ful, __ where Your
2. *See additional lyrics*

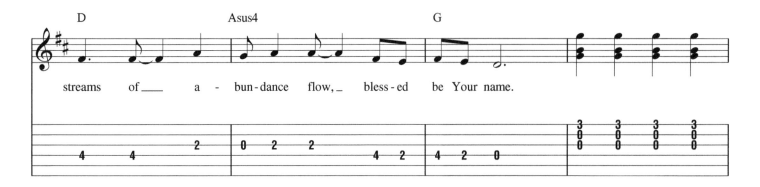

streams   of ____ a - bun - dance   flow, __ bless - ed   be Your name.

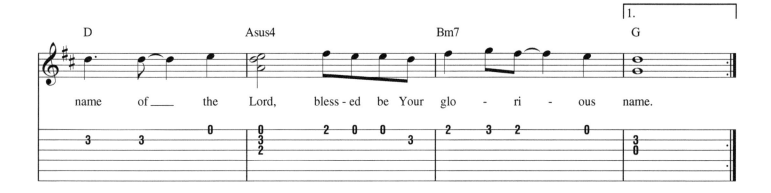

name of ___ the Lord, bless - ed be Your glo - ri - ous name.

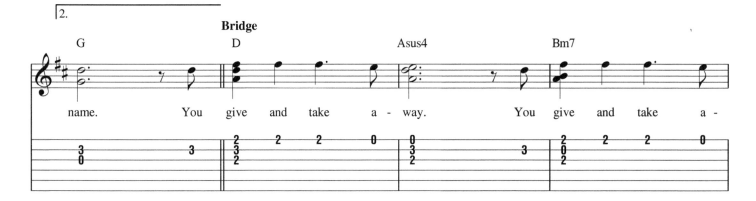

Bridge

name. You give and take a - way. You give and take a -

To Coda

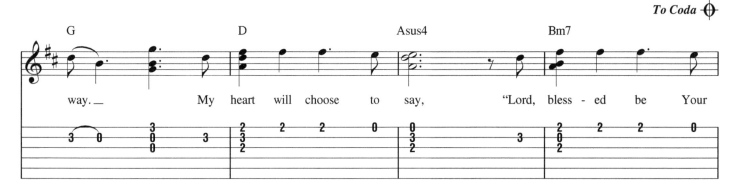

way. ___ My heart will choose to say, "Lord, bless - ed be Your

Pre-Chorus

name." _____ Ev - 'ry bless - ing You pour out I'll ___

*Let chord ring, next 2 meas.

turn back to praise. When the dark - ness clos - es in, Lord, _

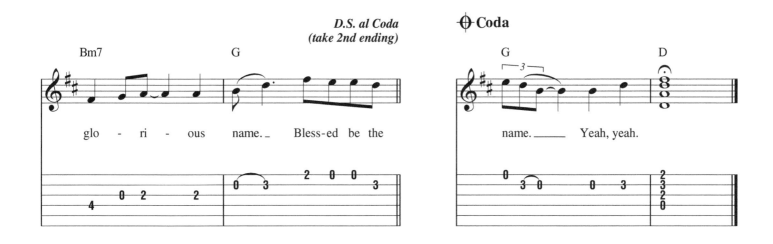

Additional Lyrics

2. Blessed be Your name when the sun's shining down on me,
   When the world's all as it should be, blessed be Your name.
   Blessed be Your name on the road marked with suffering.
   Though there's pain in the offering, blessed be Your name.

Glory to God Forever

Words and Music by Steve Fee and Vicky Beeching

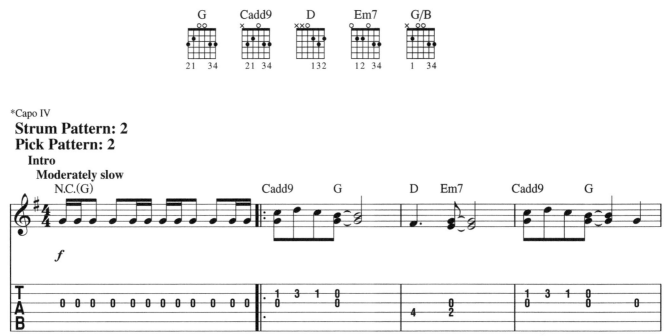

*Capo IV

Strum Pattern: 2

Pick Pattern: 2

Intro

Moderately slow

*Optional: To match recording, place capo at 4th fret.

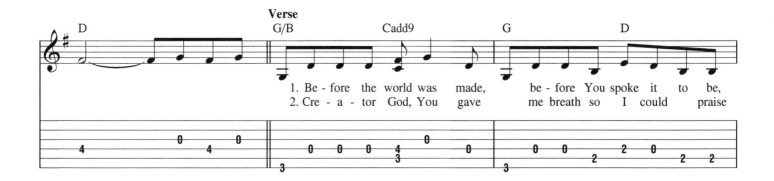

1. Be - fore the world was made, be - fore You spoke it to be,
2. Cre - a - tor God, You gave me breath so I could praise

You were the King of kings, yeah, You were, yeah, You were. And now You're reign-ing still,
Your great and match-less name all my days, all my days. So let my whole life be

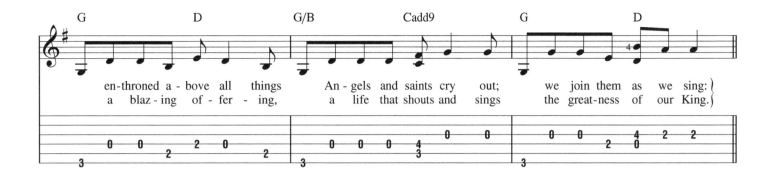

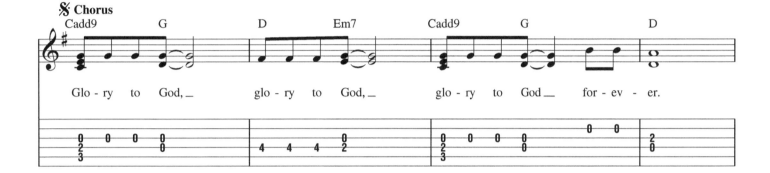

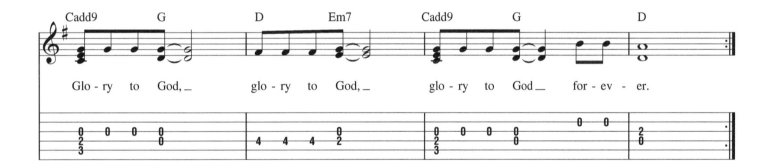

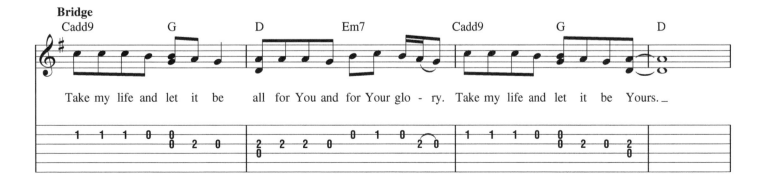

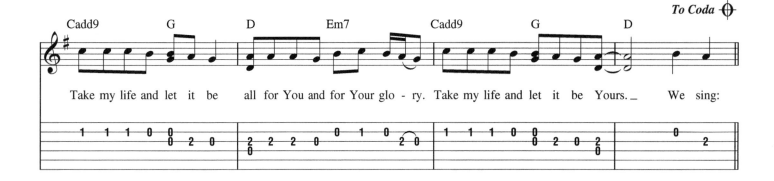

Take my life and let it be   all for You and for Your glo - ry. Take my life and let it be Yours. __   We sing:

Chorus

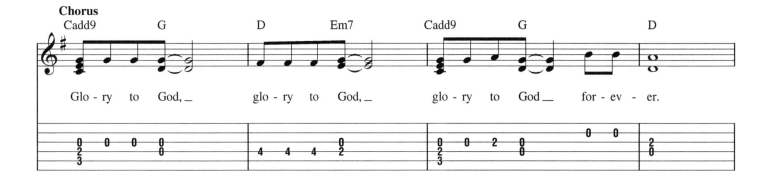

Glo - ry   to   God, __   glo - ry   to   God, __   glo - ry   to   God __   for - ev - er.

D.S. al Coda
(no repeat)

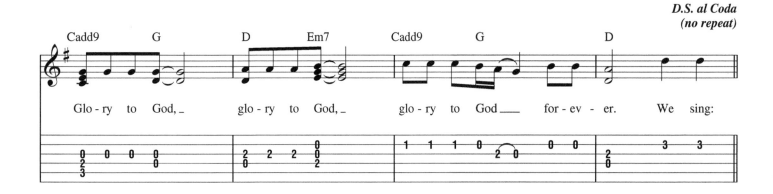

Glo - ry   to   God, __   glo - ry   to   God, __   glo - ry   to   God __   for - ev - er.   We   sing:

⊕ **Coda**
Outro
*G

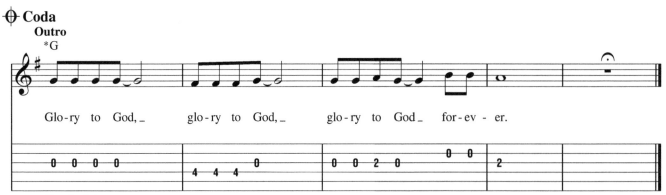

Glo - ry   to   God, __   glo - ry   to   God, __   glo - ry   to   God __   for - ev - er.

*Let chord ring.

God of This City

Words and Music by Aaron Boyd, Peter Comfort, Richard Bleakley, Peter Kernaghan, Andrew McCann and Ian Jordan

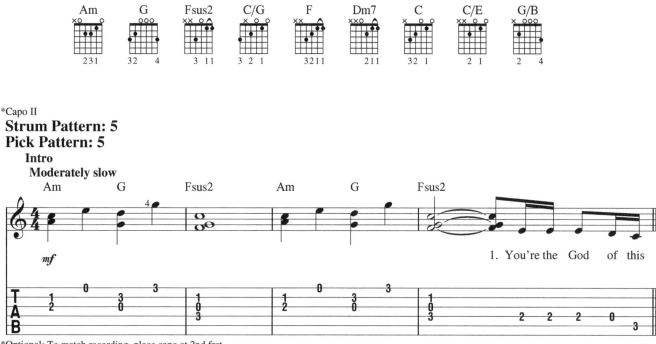

*Capo II

Strum Pattern: 5
Pick Pattern: 5

Intro
Moderately slow

1. You're the God of this

*Optional: To match recording, place capo at 2nd fret.

Verse

(2.) cit - y, _____ You're the King of these peo - ple, _____ You're the Lord of this na - tion, _____ You

are. _____ You're the light in this dark - ness, _____ You're the hope to the hope - less, _____ You're the peace to the

rest - less, _____ You are.   There   is   no one like our _____ God. _____   There   is   no one like our _____

*2nd time, substitute C.

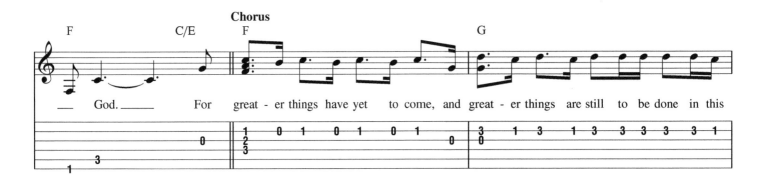

_____ God. _____   For   great - er things have yet   to come, and great - er things are still   to be done   in this

cit - y. _____   Great - er things have yet   to come, and great - er things are still   to be done   in this

cit - y. _____   2. You're the God of this   Great - er things have yet   to come, and

great - er things are still   to be done here.

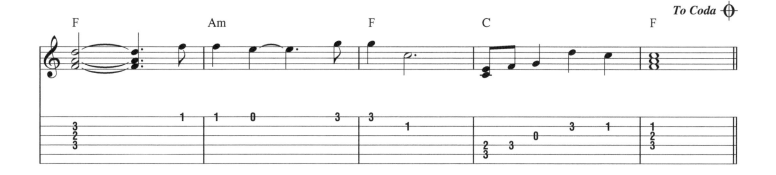

Pre-Chorus

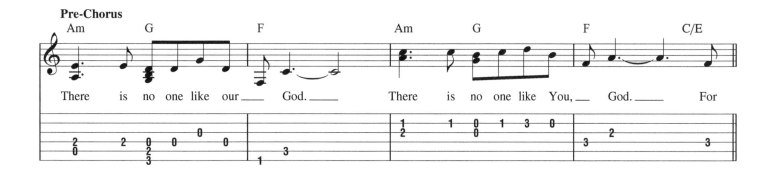

There is no one like our ___ God. ___ There is no one like You, ___ God. ___ For

Chorus

great - er things have yet to come, and great - er things are still to be done in this cit - y. _____

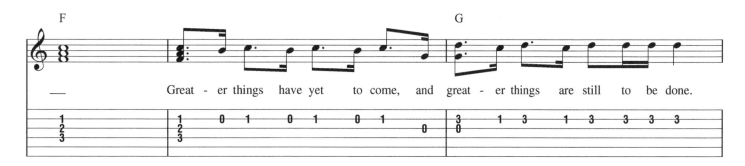

___ Great - er things have yet to come, and great - er things are still to be done.

⊕ **Coda**

D.S. al Coda
(take 2nd ending)

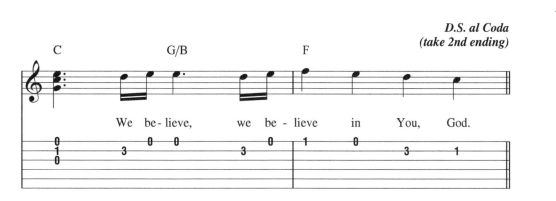

We be - lieve, we be - lieve in You, God.

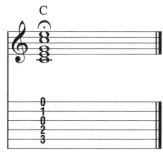

God of Wonders

Words and Music by Marc Byrd and Steve Hindalong

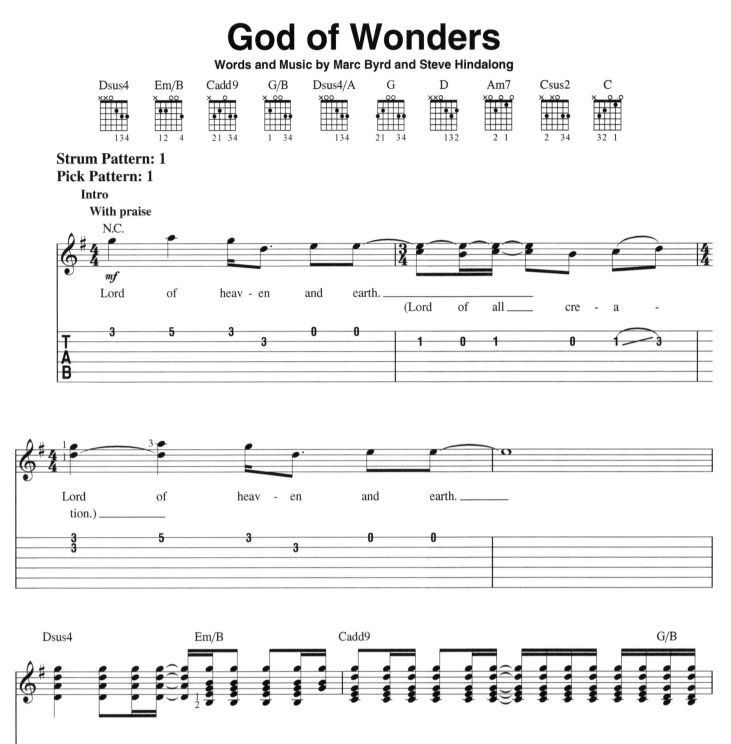

Strum Pattern: 1

Pick Pattern: 1

Intro

With praise

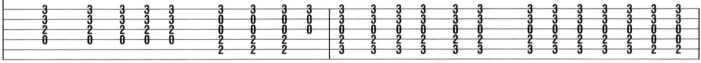

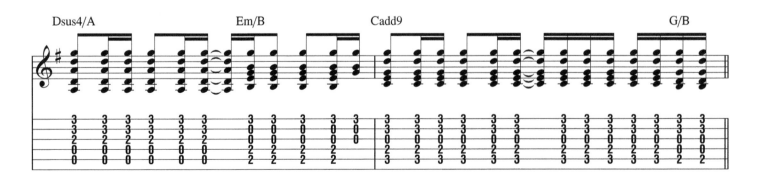

Verse

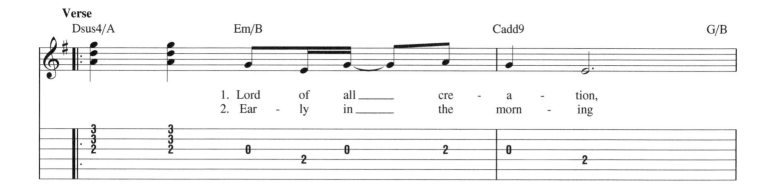

1. Lord of all _____ cre - a - tion,
2. Ear - ly in _____ the morn - ing

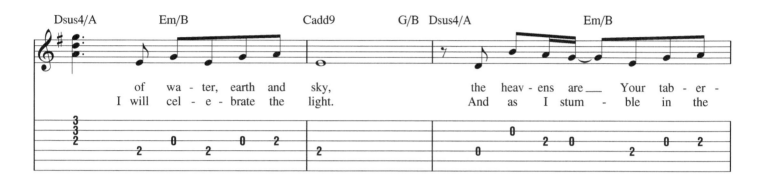

of wa - ter, earth and sky,   the heav - ens are _____ Your tab - er -
I will cel - e - brate the light.   And as I stum - ble in the

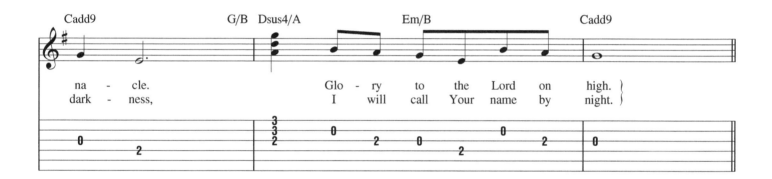

na - cle.   Glo - ry to the Lord on high.
dark - ness,   I will call Your name by night.

Chorus

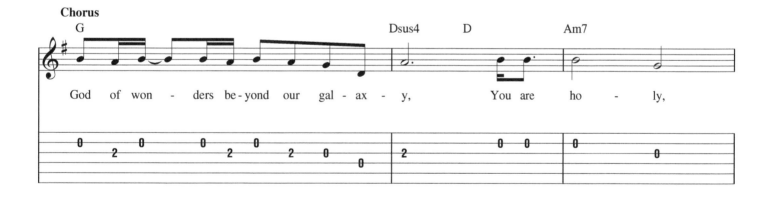

God of won - ders be - yond our gal - ax - y,   You are ho - ly,

ho - ly. The u - ni - verse _ de - clares Your maj - es - ty.   You are

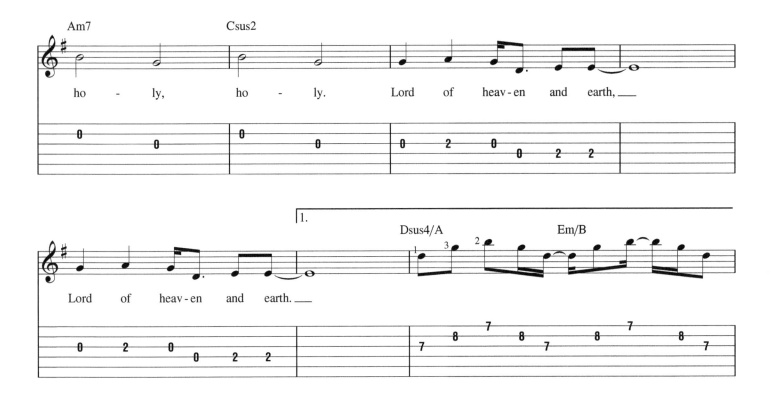

ho - ly, ho - ly. Lord of heav-en and earth, ___

1.

Lord of heav-en and earth. ___

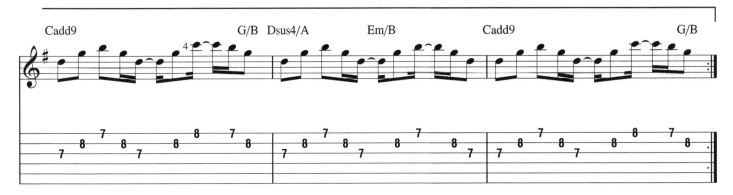

2.

Bridge

Hal - le - lu - jah to the Lord of heav - en and earth.

Hal - le - lu - jah to the Lord of heav - en and earth.

Guitar Solo

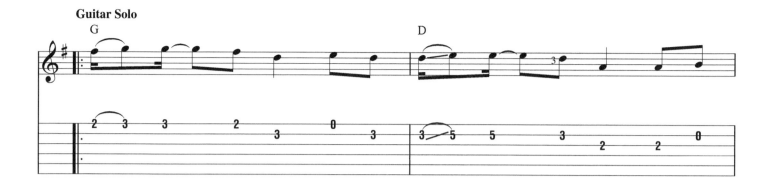

Chorus

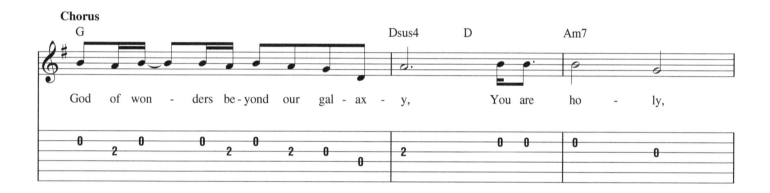

God of won - ders be - yond our gal - ax - y, You are ho - ly,

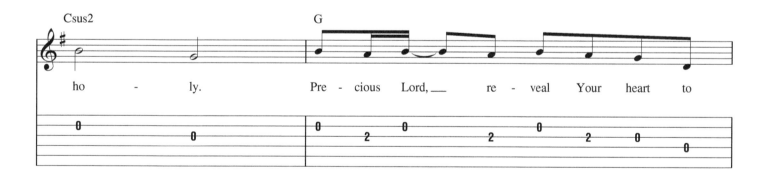

ho - ly. Pre - cious Lord, __ re - veal Your heart to

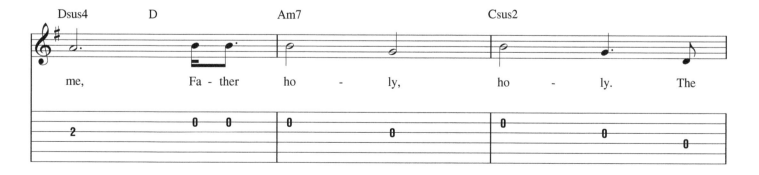

me, Fa - ther ho - ly, ho - ly. The

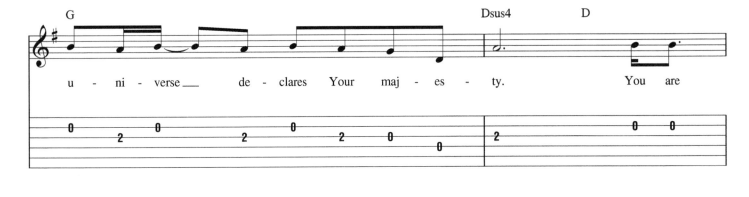

u - ni - verse___ de - clares Your maj - es - ty. You are

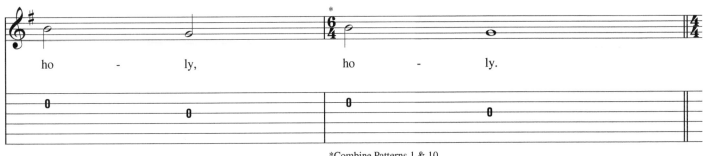

ho - ly, ho - ly,

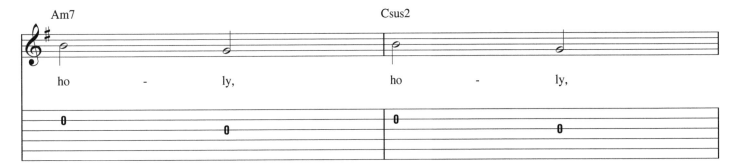

ho - ly, ho - ly.

*Combine Patterns 1 & 10

Outro

Play 5 times

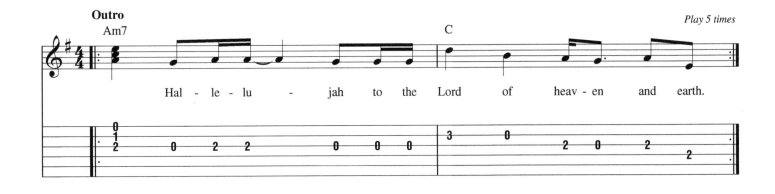

Hal - le - lu - jah to the Lord of heav - en and earth.

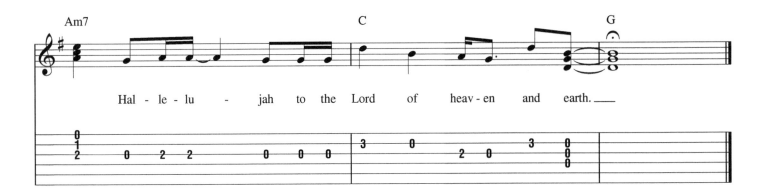

Hal - le - lu - jah to the Lord of heav - en and earth.___

God You Reign

Words and Music by Lincoln Brewster and Mia Fieldes

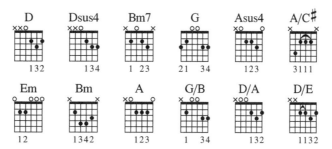

Strum Pattern: 5
Pick Pattern: 4

Intro
Moderately

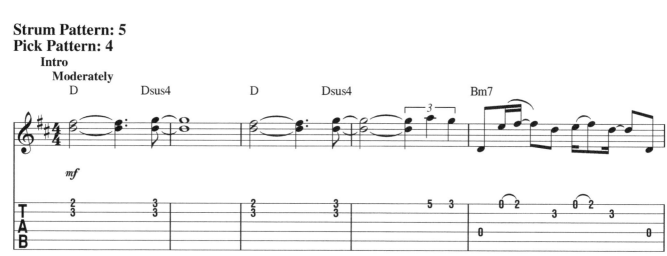

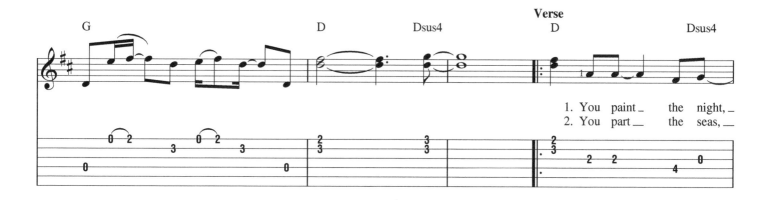

1. You paint the night,
2. You part the seas,

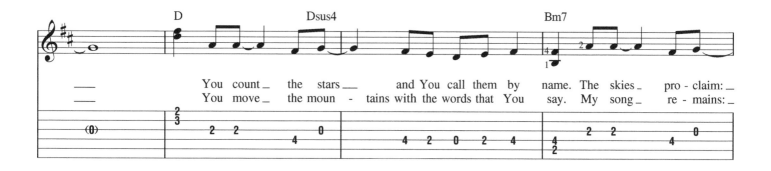

You count the stars and You call them by name. The skies pro-claim:
You move the moun - tains with the words that You say. My song re - mains:

God, You reign. _
God, You reign. _

Your glo - ry shines, _
You hold _ my life, _____

You teach _ the sun
You know _ my heart _

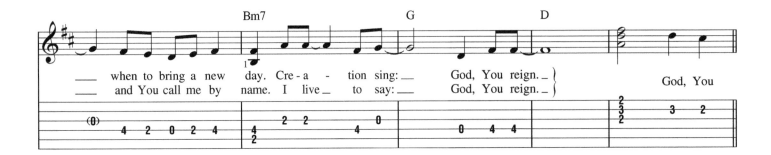

_ when to bring a new day. Cre - a - tion sing: _ God, You reign. _)
_ and You call me by name. I live _ to say: _ God, You reign. _)

God, You

𝄋 Chorus

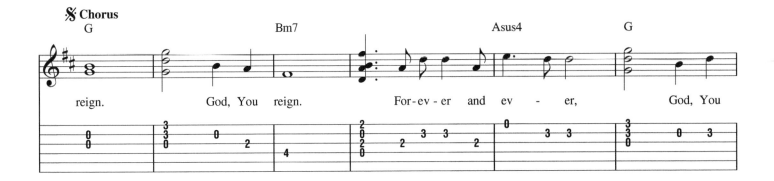

reign.

God, You reign.

For - ev - er and ev - er,

God, You

1.

2.

reign. _____

reign. Whoa, _ God, You reign.

God, You reign.

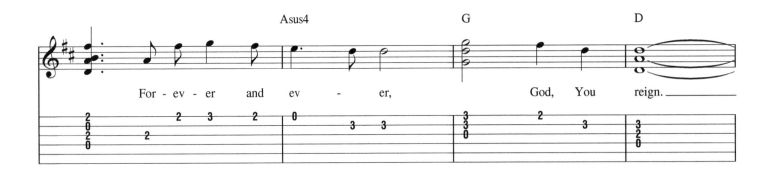

For - ev - er and ev - er,

God, You reign. _____

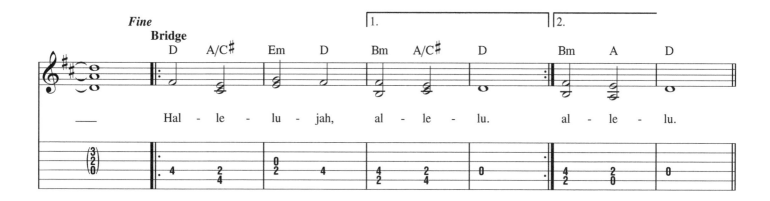

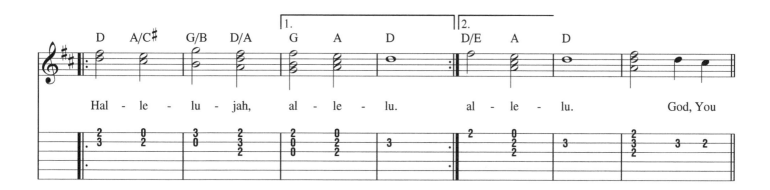

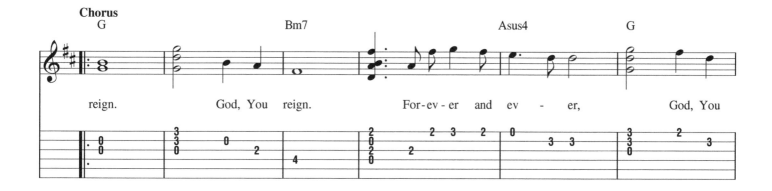

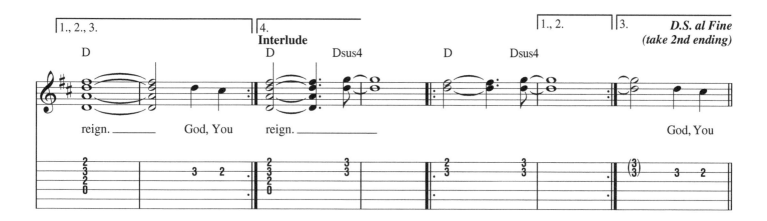

Here I Am to Worship

Words and Music by Tim Hughes

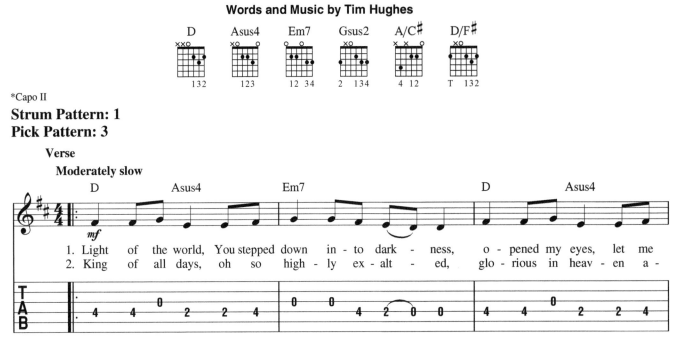

*Capo II

Strum Pattern: 1
Pick Pattern: 3

Verse

Moderately slow

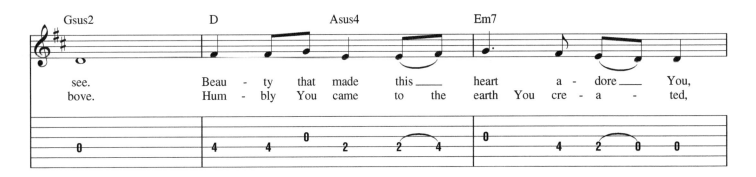

1. Light of the world, You stepped down in-to dark - ness, o - pened my eyes, let me
2. King of all days, oh so high - ly ex - alt - ed, glo - rious in heav - en a -

*Optional: To match recording, place capo at 2nd fret.

see. Beau - ty that made this ___ heart a - dore ___ You,
bove. Hum - bly You came to the earth You cre - a - ted,

hope of a life spent with You.
all for love's sake be - came poor.

Here I am to

Chorus

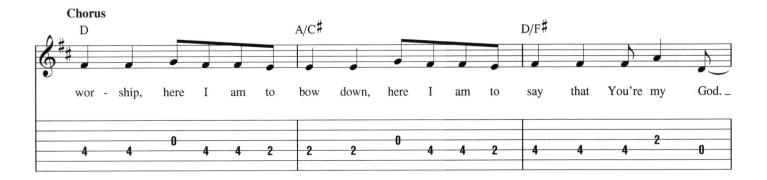

wor - ship, here I am to bow down, here I am to say that You're my God. ___

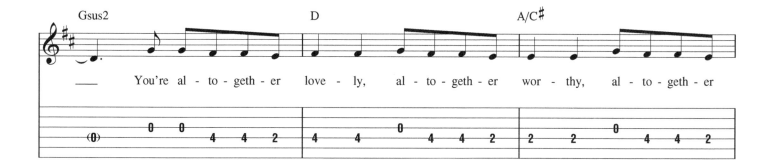

You're al - to - geth - er love - ly, al - to - geth - er wor - thy, al - to - geth - er

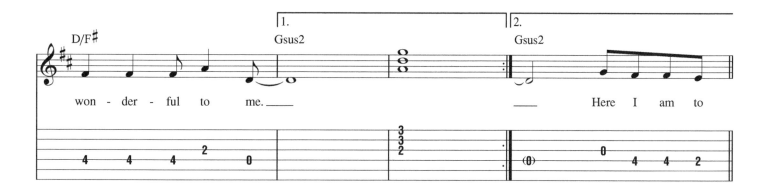

won - der - ful to me.____ ____ Here I am to

Chorus

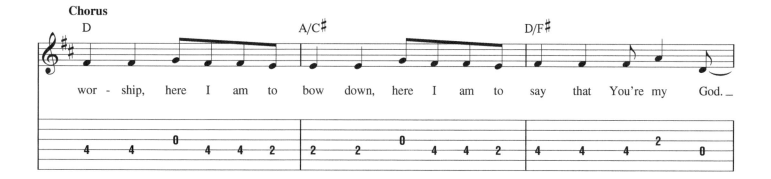

wor - ship, here I am to bow down, here I am to say that You're my God.__

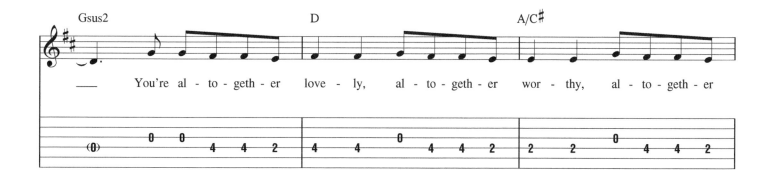

You're al - to - geth - er love - ly, al - to - geth - er wor - thy, al - to - geth - er

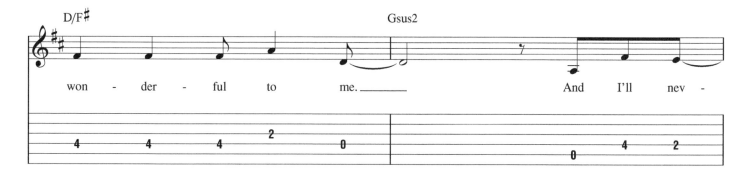

won - der - ful to me._____ And I'll nev -

Bridge

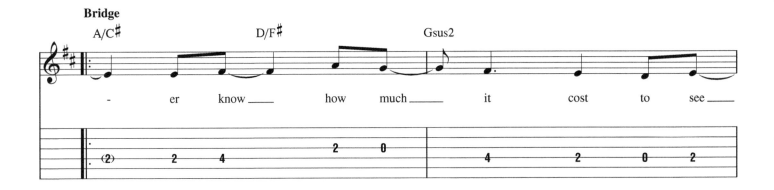

-er know ____ how much ____ it cost to see ____

____ my sin ____ up - on ____ that cross. I'll nev - ____ that cross. ____

Outro-Chorus

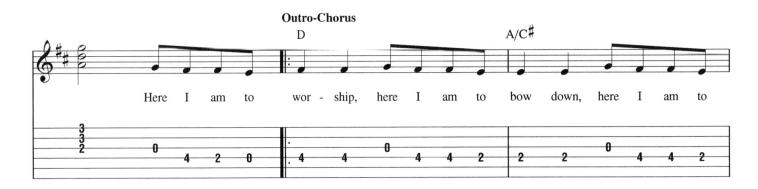

Here I am to wor - ship, here I am to bow down, here I am to

say that You're my God. ____ You're al - to - geth - er love - ly, al - to - geth - er

Repeat and fade

wor - thy, al - to - geth - er won - der - ful to me. ____ Here I am to

Hosanna
(Praise Is Rising)

Words and Music by Paul Baloche and Brenton Brown

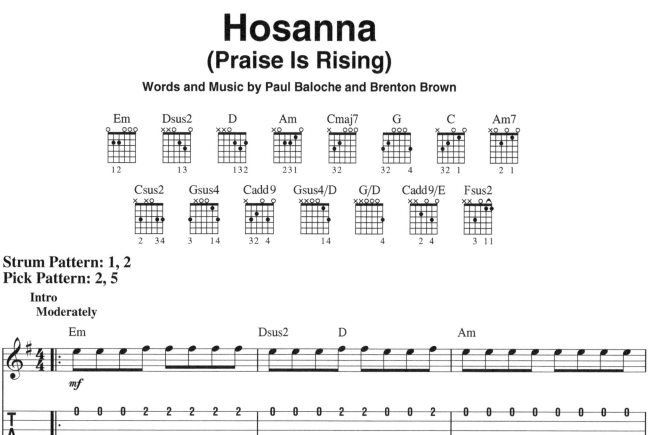

Strum Pattern: 1, 2
Pick Pattern: 2, 5

Intro
Moderately

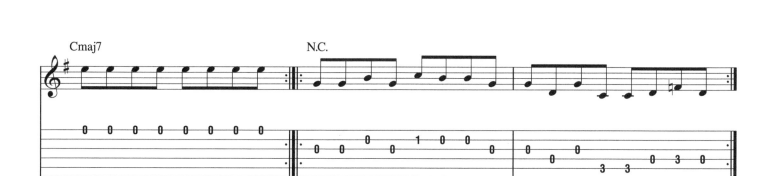

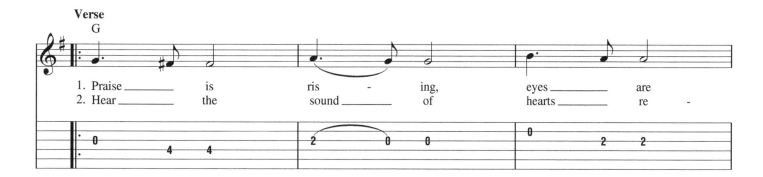

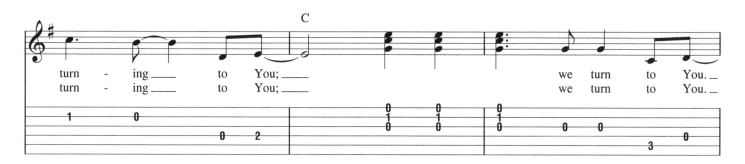

1. Praise _____ is ris - ing, eyes _____ are
2. Hear _____ the sound _____ of hearts _____ re -

turn - ing _____ to You; _____ we turn to You. ___
turn - ing _____ to You; _____ we turn to You. ___

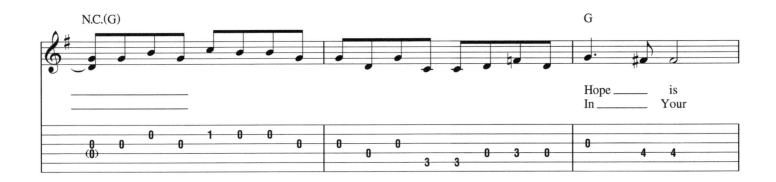

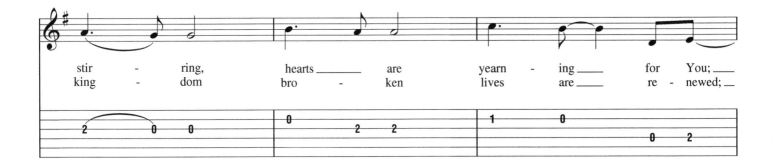

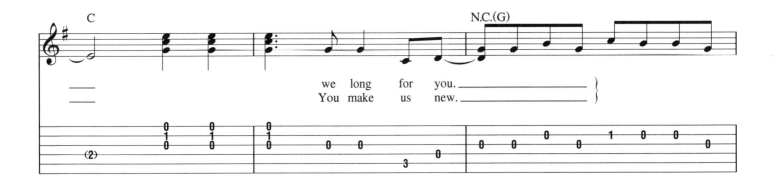

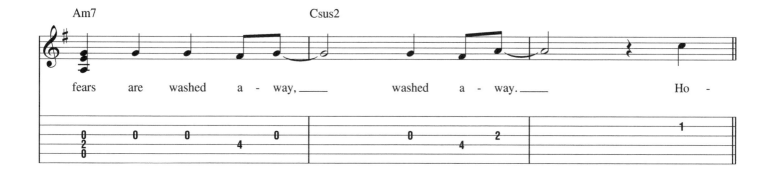

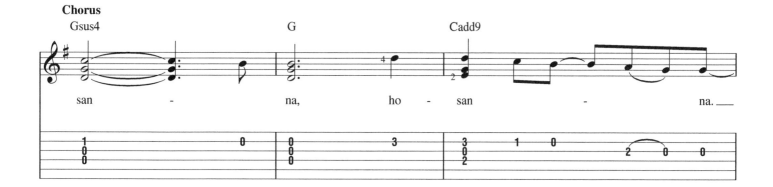

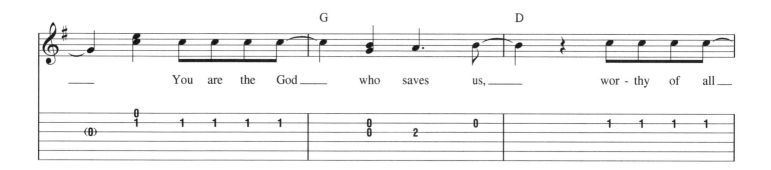

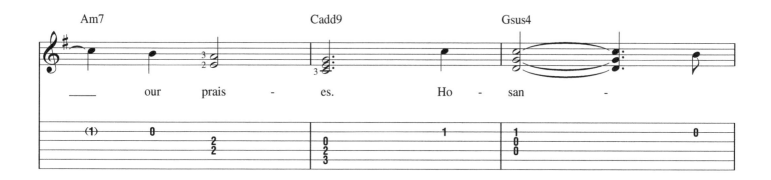

us. We wel - come You here, ___ Lord Je - sus. ___

sus. ___

Bridge

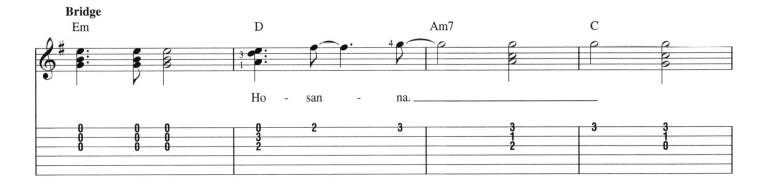

Ho - san - na. ___

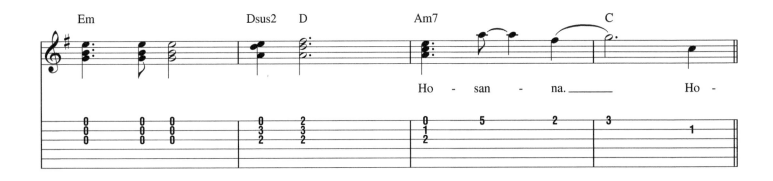

Ho - san - na. ___ Ho -

Chorus

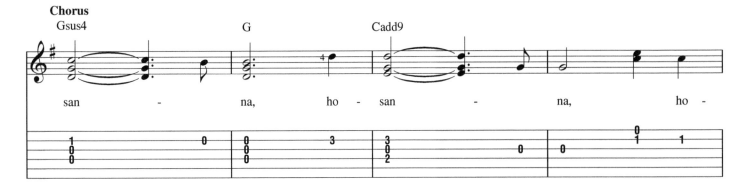

san - na, ho - san - na, ho -

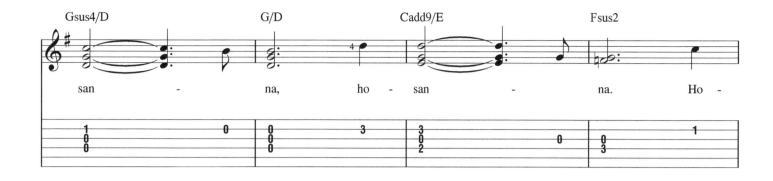

san - na, ho - san - na. Ho -

san - na, ho - san - na. ___ Come, have Your way ___

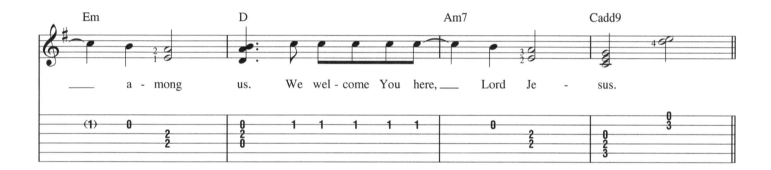

___ a - mong us. We wel - come You here, ___ Lord Je - sus.

Outro

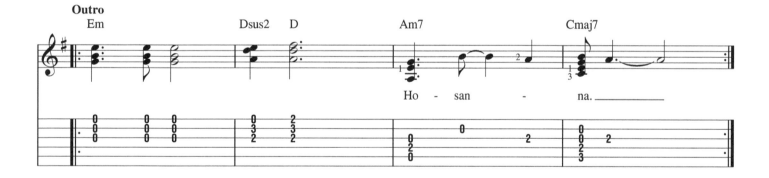

Ho - san - na. ___

How Deep the Father's Love for Us

Words and Music by Stuart Townend

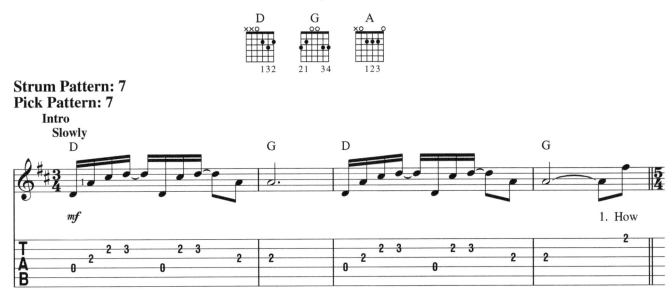

Strum Pattern: 7
Pick Pattern: 7

Intro
Slowly

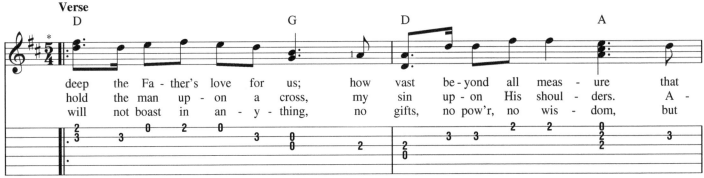

1. How

Verse

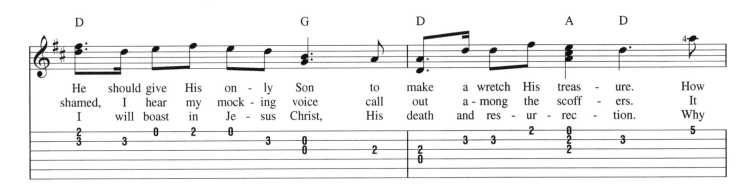

deep the Fa-ther's love for us; how vast be-yond all meas-ure that
hold the man up-on a cross, my sin up-on His shoul-ders. A-
will not boast in an-y-thing, no gifts, no pow'r, no wis-dom, but

*Combine patterns 7 & 10 for ⅝meas.

He should give His on-ly Son to make a wretch His treas-ure. How
shamed, I hear my mock-ing voice call out a-mong the scoff-ers. It
I will boast in Je-sus Christ, His death and res-ur-rec-tion. Why

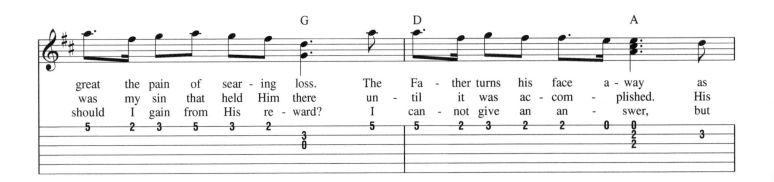

great the pain of sear-ing loss. The Fa-ther turns his face a-way as
was my sin that held Him there un-til it was ac-com-plished. His
should I gain from His re-ward? I can-not give an an-swer, but

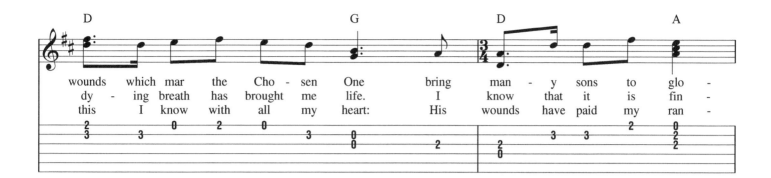

wounds which mar the Cho - sen One bring man - y sons to glo -
dy - ing breath has brought me life. I know that it is fin -
this I know with all my heart: His wounds have paid my ran -

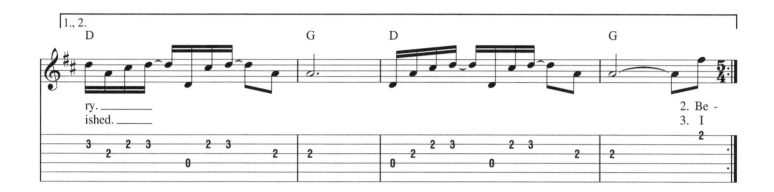

1., 2.

ry. _____
ished. _____
2. Be -
3. I

3.

Outro

som. _____ Why should I gain from His re - ward? I can - not give an an - swer, but

*Use pattern 10

this I know with all my heart: His wounds have paid my ran - som. _____

How He Loves

Words and Music by John Mark McMillan

*Piano arr. for gtr., next 8 meas.

**Sung one octave lower.

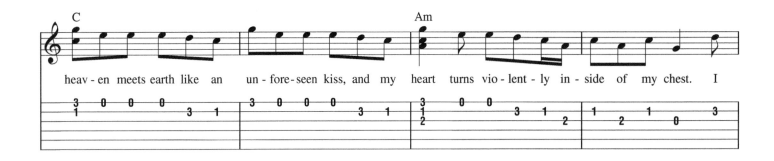

heav-en meets earth like an un-fore-seen kiss, and my heart turns vio-lent-ly in-side of my chest. I

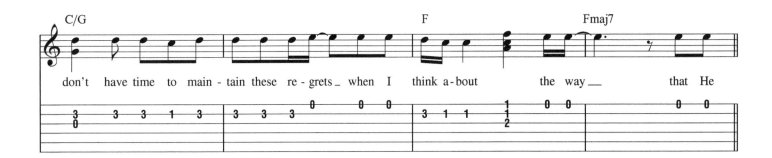

don't have time to main-tain these re-grets_ when I think a-bout the way_ that He

To Coda ⊕

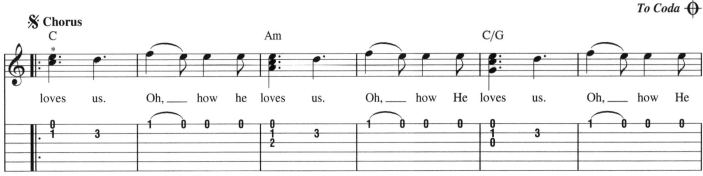

%. **Chorus**

loves us. Oh,_ how he loves us. Oh,_ how He loves us. Oh,_ how He

*3rd time, sung one octave lower till end.

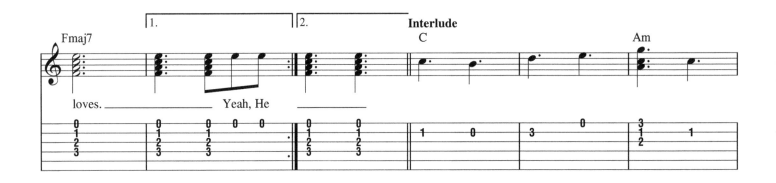

|1. |2.   **Interlude**

loves. _____ Yeah, He _____

⊕ **Coda**

D.S. al Coda

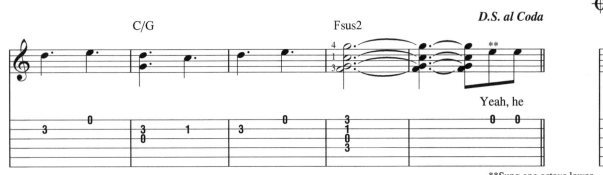

Yeah, he   loves.

**Sung one octave lower.

I Am Free

Words and Music by Jon Egan

Strum Pattern: 2, 6
Pick Pattern: 2, 5

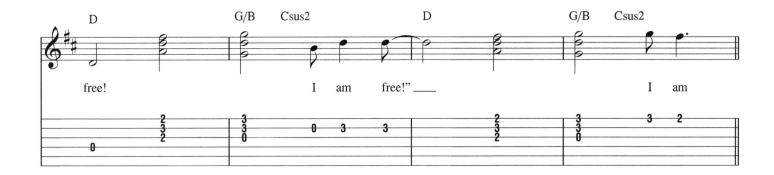

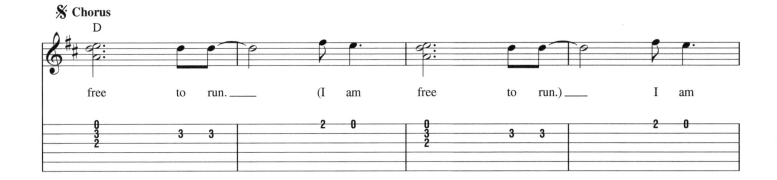

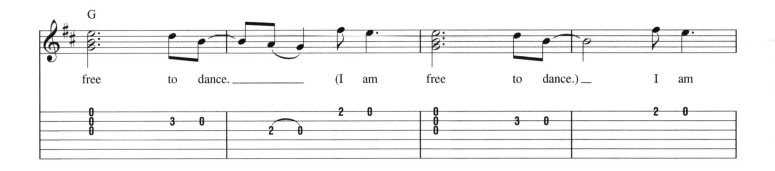

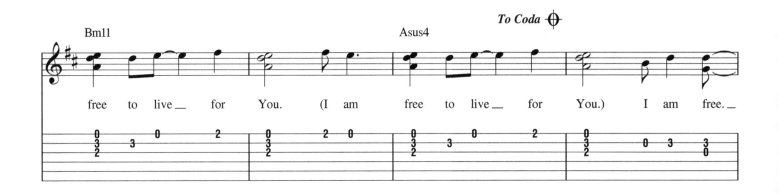

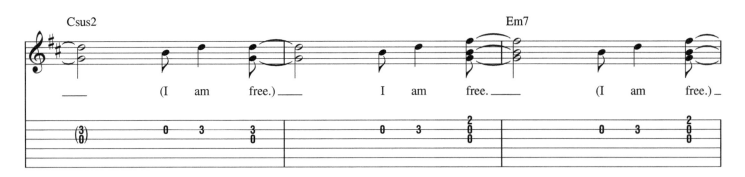

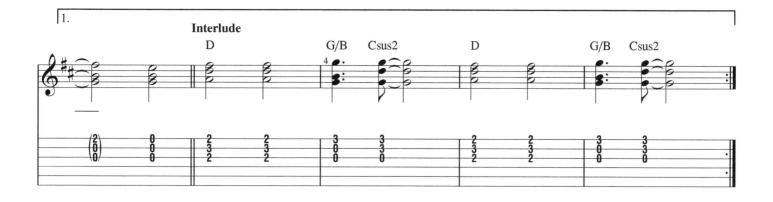

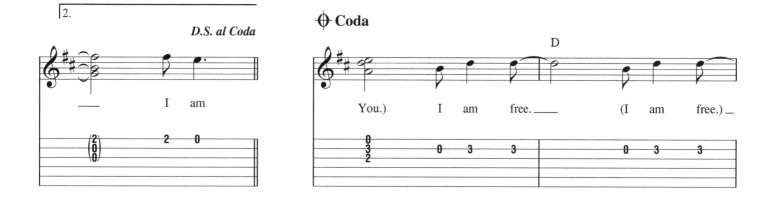

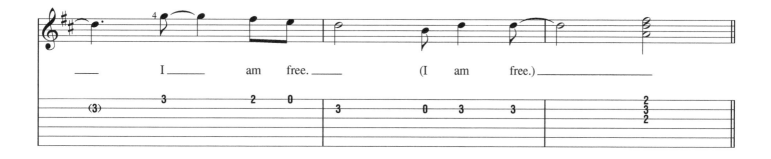

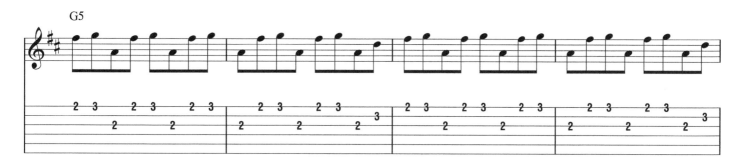

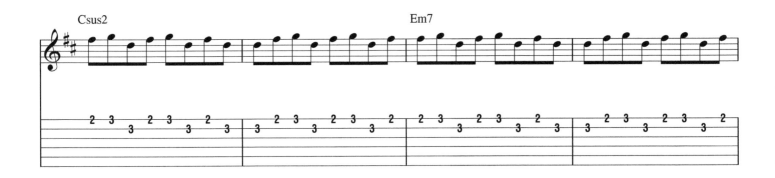

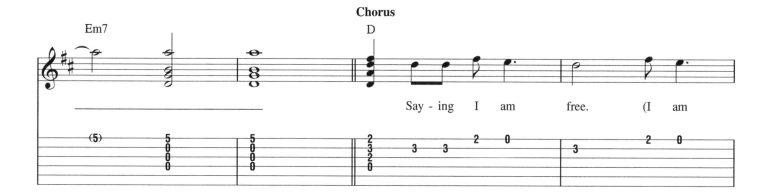

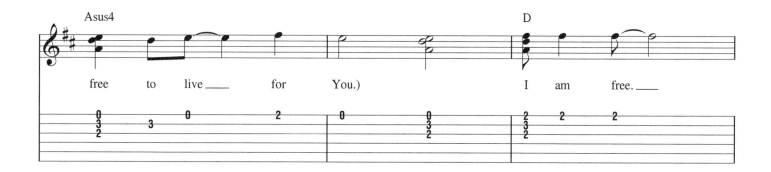

I Give You My Heart

Words and Music by Reuben Morgan

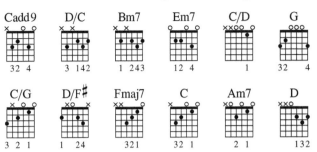

Strum Pattern: 3
Pick Pattern: 4

Intro
Moderately slow

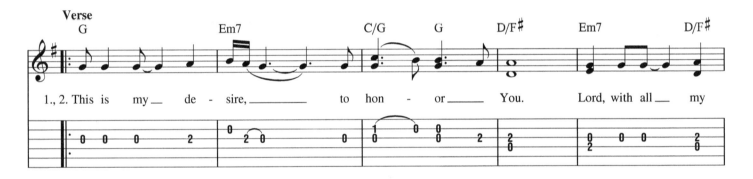

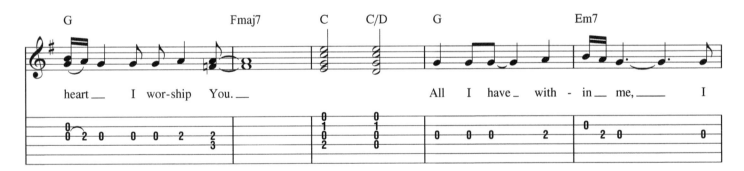

1., 2. This is my de - sire, to hon - or You. Lord, with all my

heart I wor-ship You. All I have with - in me, I

give You praise. All that I a - dore is in You.

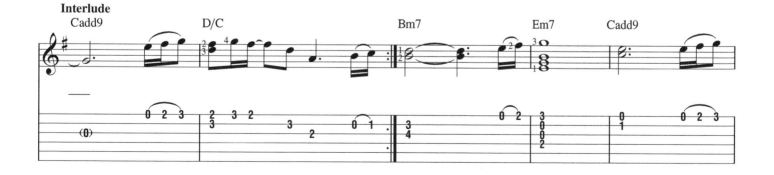

Lead Me to the Cross

Words and Music by Brooke Fraser

*Capo II

Strum Pattern: 3
Pick Pattern: 3

Intro
Slowly

*Optional: To match recording, place capo at 2nd fret.

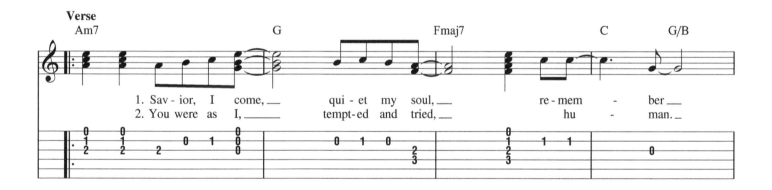

Verse

1. Sav - ior, I come, __ qui - et my soul, __ re - mem - ber __
2. You were as I, __ tempt - ed and tried, __ hu - man. __

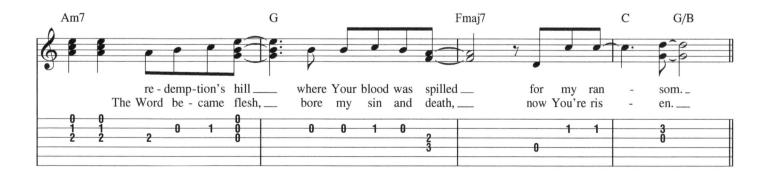

re - demp - tion's hill __ where Your blood was spilled __ for my ran - som.
The Word be - came flesh, __ bore my sin and death, __ now You're ris - en. __

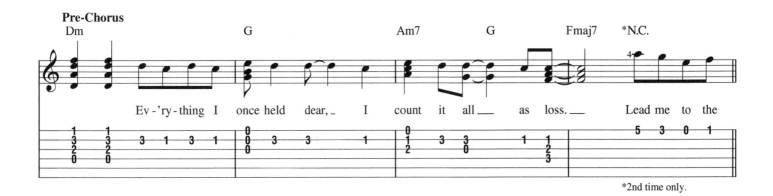

Pre-Chorus

Ev-'ry-thing I once held dear,_ I count it all_ as loss._ Lead me to the

*2nd time only.

Chorus

cross where Your love poured out._ Bring me to my knees, Lord, I lay me down._ Rid me of my-

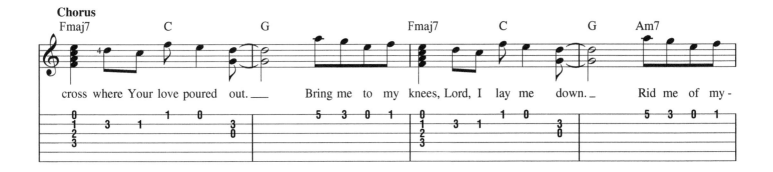

self, I be-long to You._ Oh, lead me,_ lead me to the cross._

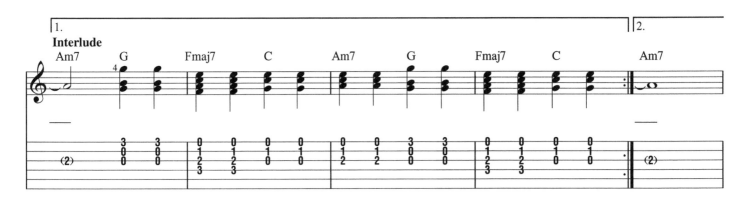

Interlude

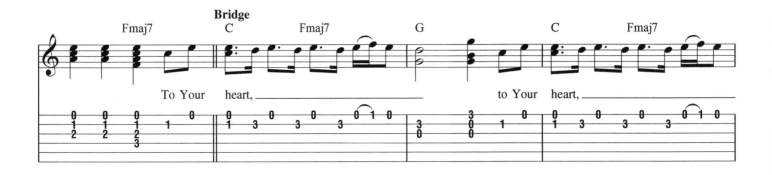

Bridge

To Your heart,_ to Your heart,_

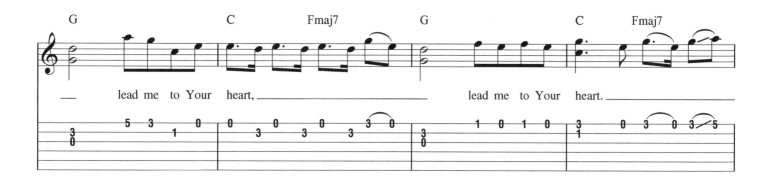

lead me to Your heart,_____ lead me to Your heart._____

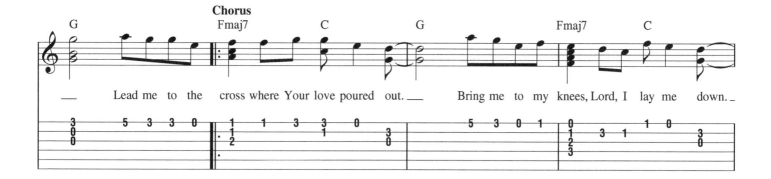

Chorus

Lead me to the cross where Your love poured out. ___ Bring me to my knees, Lord, I lay me down._

Rid me of my-self, I be-long to You.___ Oh, lead me,_____ lead _

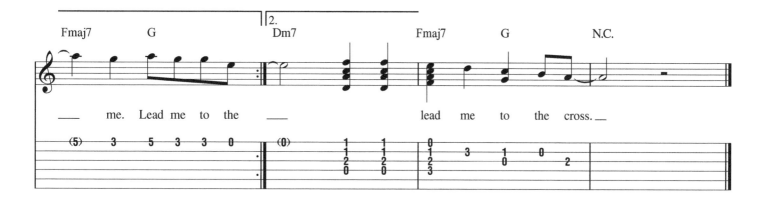

___ me. Lead me to the ___ lead me to the cross. ___

I Will Rise

Words and Music by Chris Tomlin, Jesse Reeves, Louie Giglio and Matt Maher

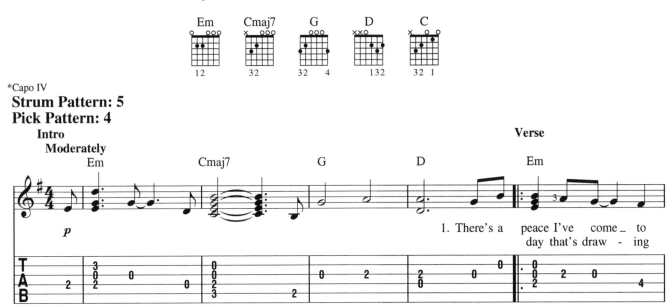

*Capo IV

Strum Pattern: 5
Pick Pattern: 4

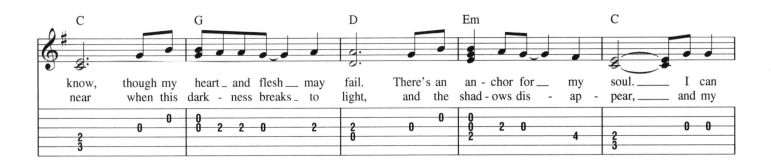

*Optional: To match recording, place capo at 4th fret.

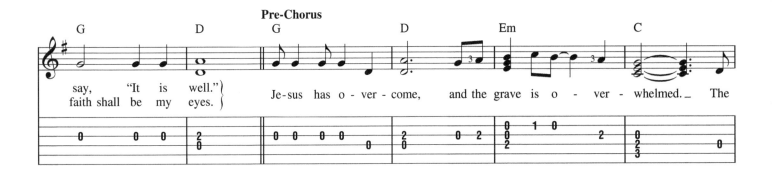

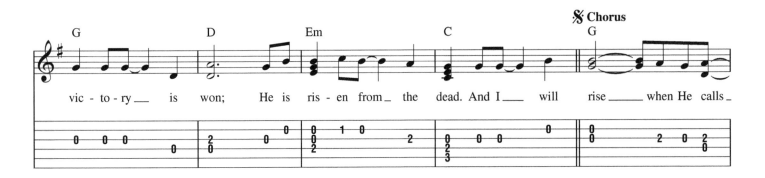

In Christ Alone

Words and Music by Keith Getty and Stuart Townend

*Optional: To match recording, place capo at 1st fret.

**Sung one octave lower, except where noted.

***Sung as written, next 4 meas.

*Sung as written, next 4 meas.

Additional Lyrics

3. There in the ground His body lay,
Light of the world by darkness slain.
Then bursting forth in glorious day,
Up from the grave He rose again.
And as He stands in victory,
Sin's curse has lost its grip on me,
For I am His and He is mine,
Bought with the precious blood of Christ.

4. No guilt in life, no fear in death,
This is the pow'r of Christ in me.
From life's first cry to final breath,
Jesus commands my destiny.
No pow'r of hell, no scheme of man
Can ever pluck me from His hand.
Till He returns or calls me home,
Here in the pow'r of Christ I'll stand.

Mighty to Save

Words and Music by Ben Fielding and Reuben Morgan

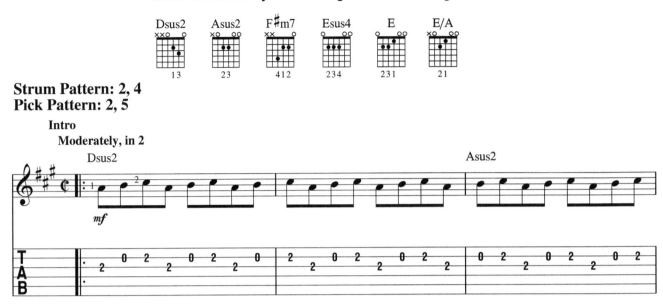

Strum Pattern: 2, 4
Pick Pattern: 2, 5

Intro
Moderately, in 2

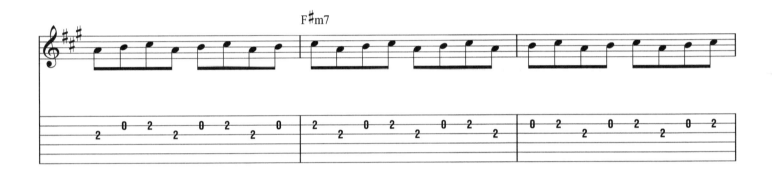

1. Well, ev'ry-one needs com-pas - sion, a
2. So take ___ me as You find ___ me,

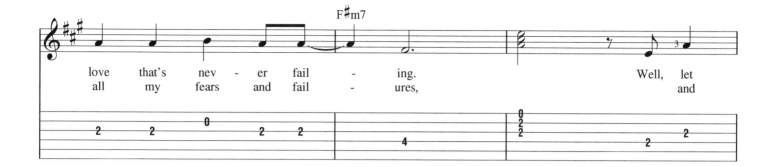

love that's nev - er fail - ing. Well, let
all my fears and fail - ures,

mer - cy fall on ___ me. ___ Well,
fill my life a - gain. ___ I

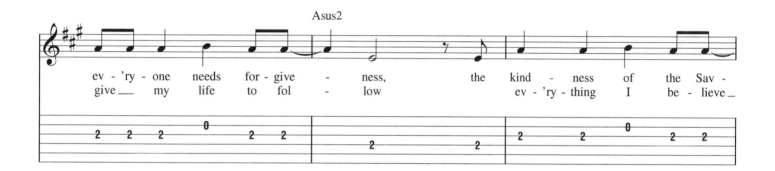

ev - 'ry - one needs for - give - ness, the kind - ness of the Sav -
give ___ my life to fol - low ev - 'ry - thing I be - lieve ___

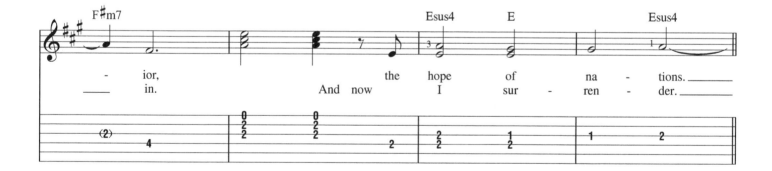

- ior, the hope of na - tions. ___
___ in. And now I sur - ren - der. ___

Pre-Chorus

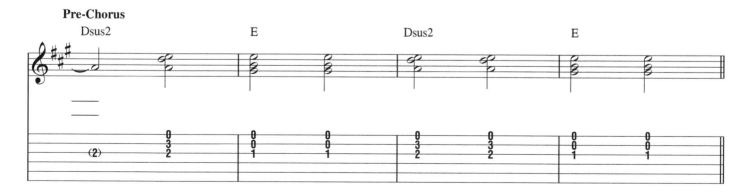

Chorus

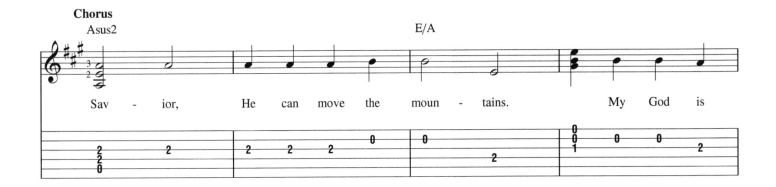

Sav - ior, He can move the moun - tains. My God is

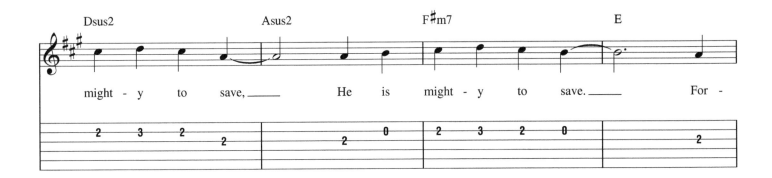

might - y to save,_____ He is might - y to save._____ For -

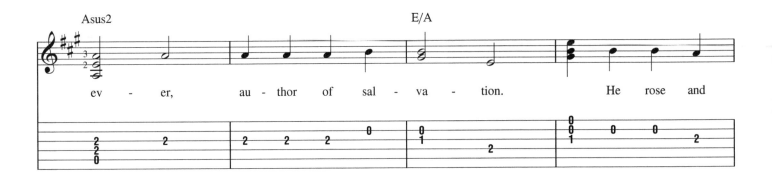

ev - er, au - thor of sal - va - tion. He rose and

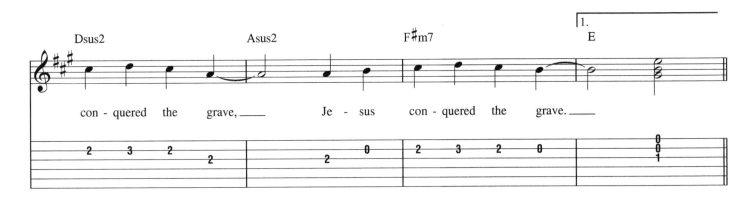

con - quered the grave,_____ Je - sus con - quered the grave._____

Interlude

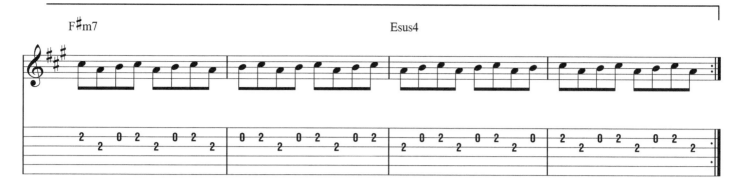

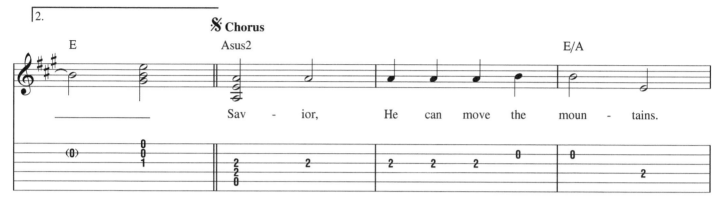

Interlude

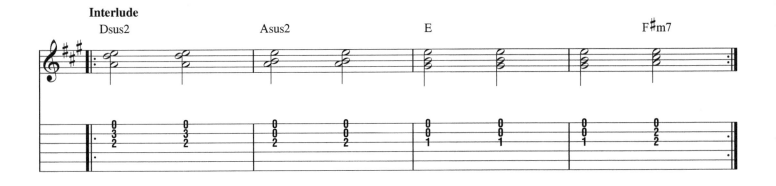

Bridge

Shine Your light and let the whole world see. Sing-in'

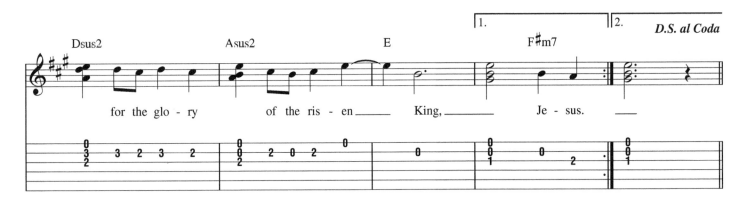

for the glo - ry of the ris - en King, Je - sus.

 Coda

Chorus

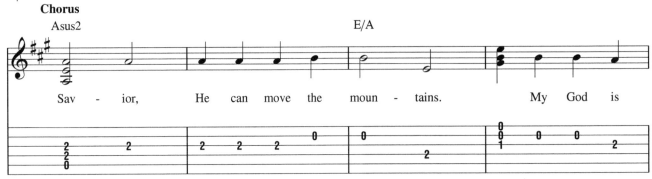

Sav - ior, He can move the moun - tains. My God is

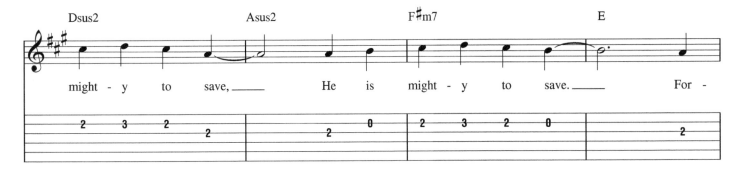

might - y to save, He is might - y to save. For -

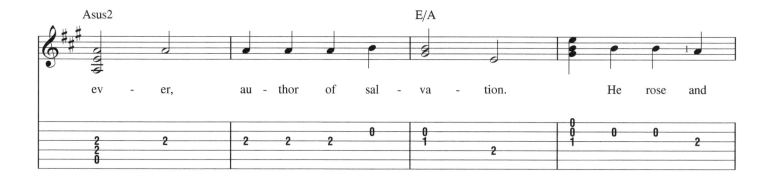

ev - er, au - thor of sal - va - tion. He rose and

con - quered the grave,___ Je - sus con - quered the grave._____

Outro

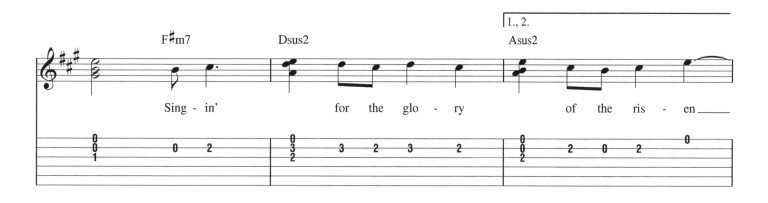

Shine Your light and let the whole world _____ see.

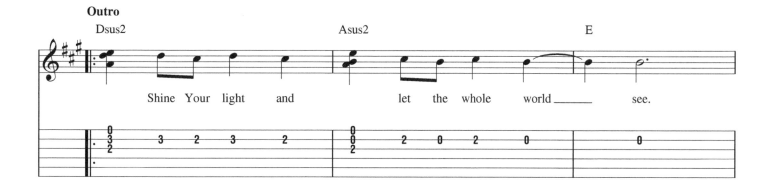

1., 2.

Sing - in' for the glo - ry of the ris - en ___

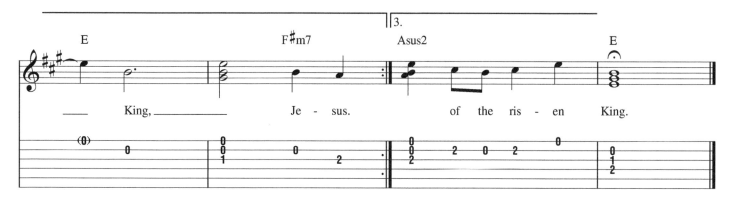

3.

___ King, _____ Je - sus. of the ris - en King.

Not to Us

Words and Music by Chris Tomlin and Jesse Reeves

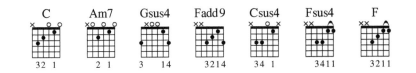

*Tune down 1/2 step:
(low to high) Eb-Ab-Db-Gb-Bb-Eb

Strum Pattern: 3, 4
Pick Pattern: 4, 5

*Optional: To match recording, tune down 1/2 step.

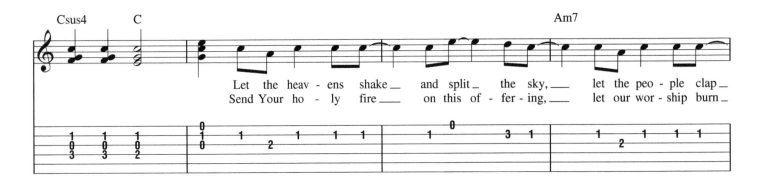

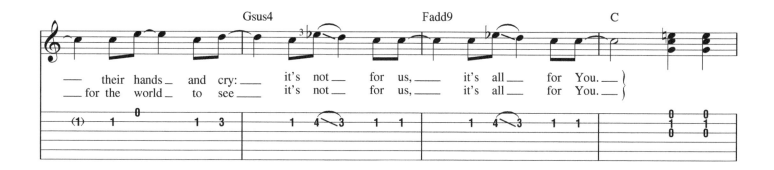

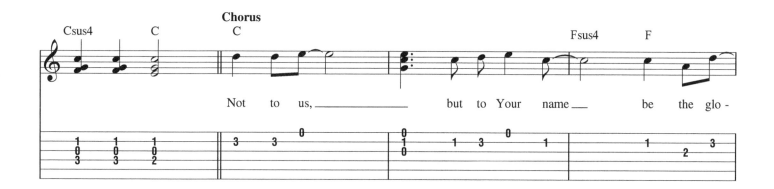

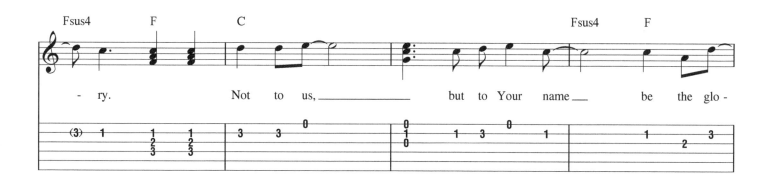

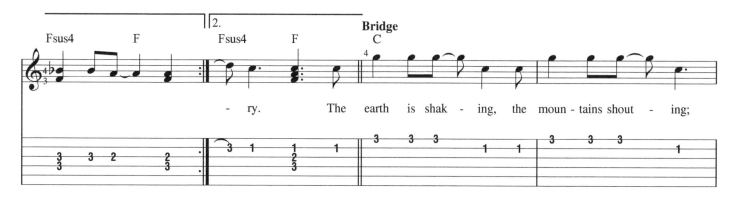

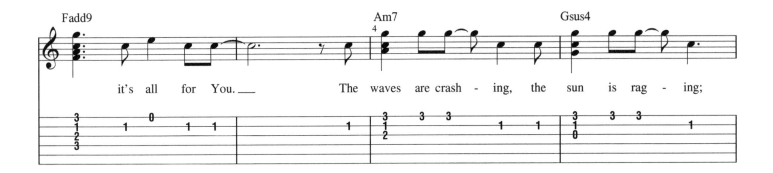

it's all for You.___ The waves are crash - ing, the sun is rag - ing;

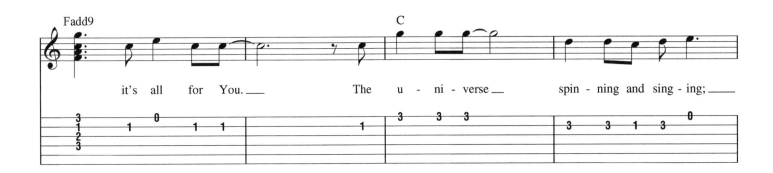

it's all for You.___ The u - ni - verse ___ spin - ning and sing - ing;___

___ it's all for You.___ Your chil - dren danc - ing, danc - ing, danc - ing;

Interlude

it's all for You,___ it's all ___ for You.___ My all ___ for You.___

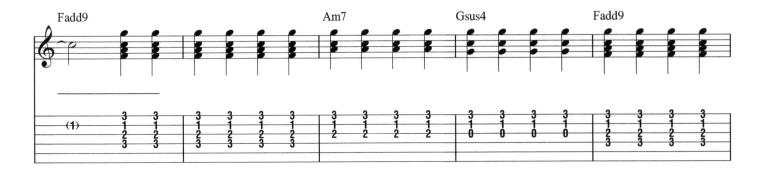

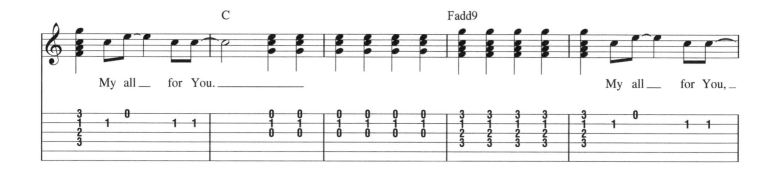

My all __ for You. _____ My all __ for You, _

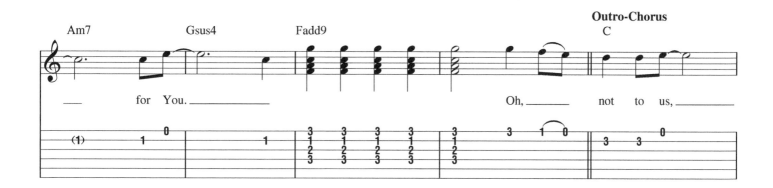

__ for You. _____ Oh, _____ not to us, _____

Outro-Chorus

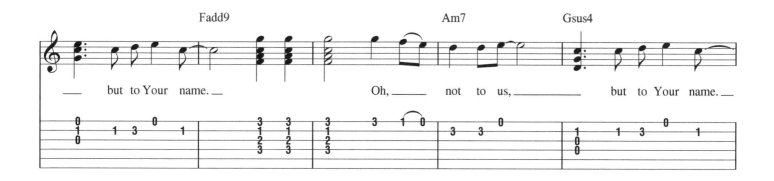

__ but to Your name. _ Oh, _____ not to us, _____ but to Your name. _

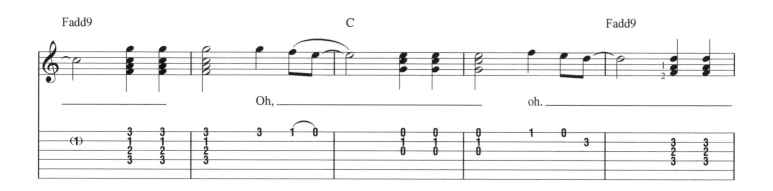

_____ Oh, _____ oh. __

__ Oh, _____ oh. _____

O Praise Him
(All This for a King)

Words and Music by David Crowder

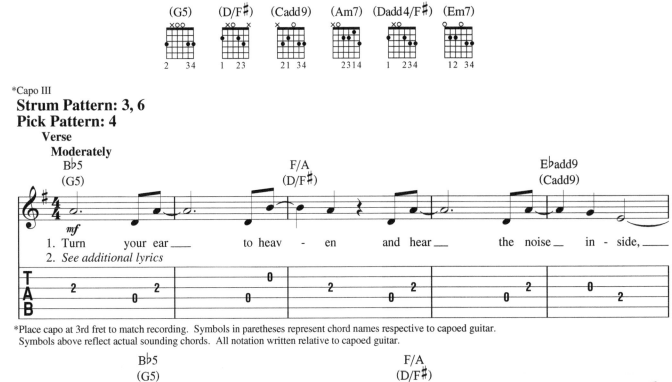

*Capo III

Strum Pattern: 3, 6
Pick Pattern: 4

Verse
Moderately

1. Turn your ear to heav - en and hear the noise in - side,
2. *See additional lyrics*

*Place capo at 3rd fret to match recording. Symbols in paretheses represent chord names respective to capoed guitar.
Symbols above reflect actual sounding chords. All notation written relative to capoed guitar.

the sound of an - gels' awe, the sound of an - gels' songs, and all

To Coda

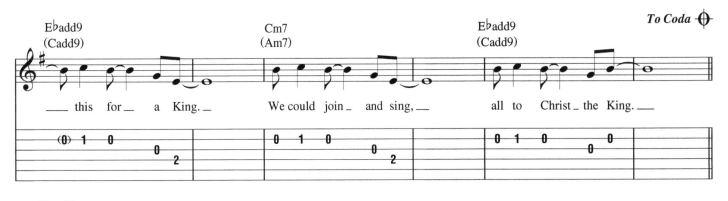

this for a King. We could join and sing, all to Christ the King.

Pre-Chorus

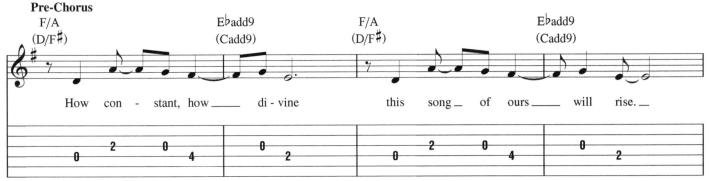

How con - stant, how di - vine this song of ours will rise.

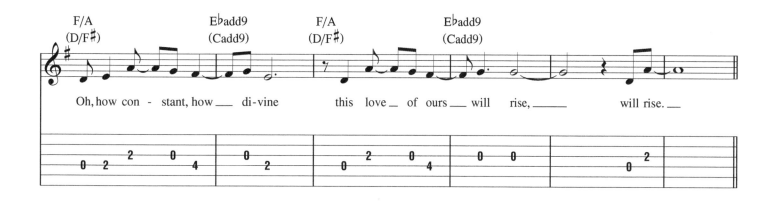

Oh, how con - stant, how ___ di - vine this love ___ of ours ___ will rise, _____ will rise. ___

Chorus

D.C. al Coda

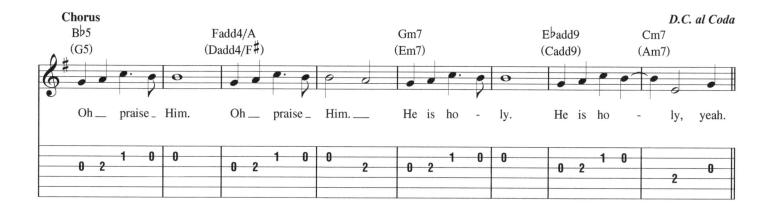

Oh ___ praise ___ Him. Oh ___ praise ___ Him. ___ He is ho - ly. He is ho - ly, yeah.

Coda

Chorus

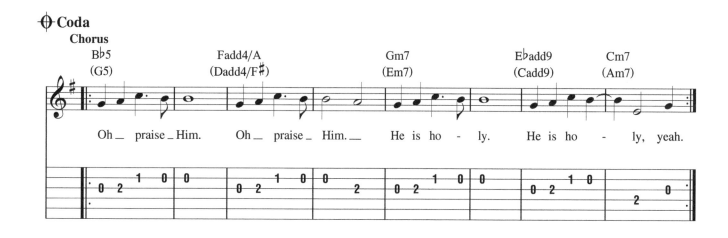

Oh ___ praise ___ Him. Oh ___ praise ___ Him. ___ He is ho - ly. He is ho - ly, yeah.

Interlude

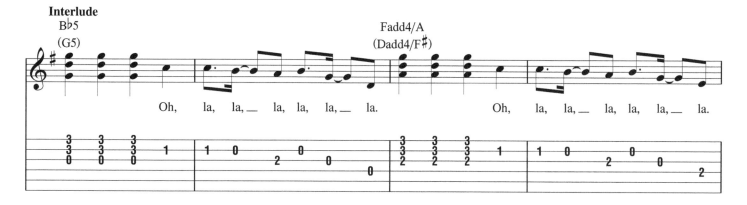

Oh, la, la, ___ la, la, la, ___ la. Oh, la, la, ___ la, la, la, ___ la.

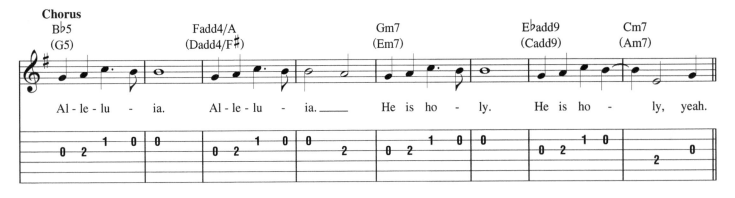

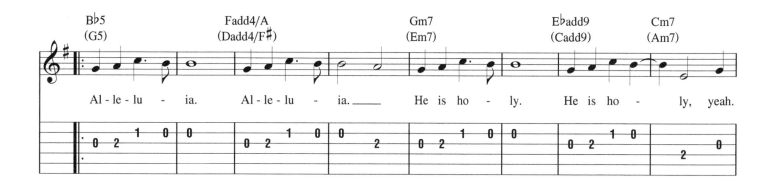

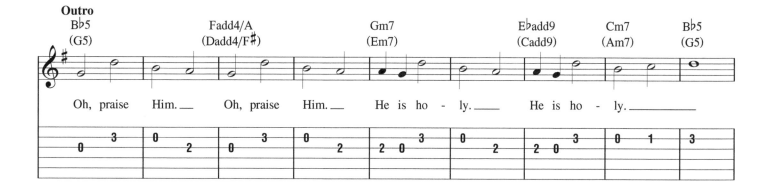

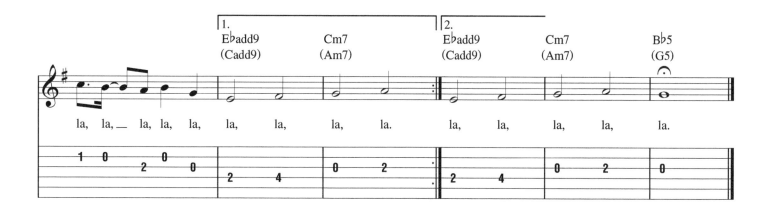

Additional Lyrics

2. Turn your gaze to heaven and raise a joyous noise
   For the sound of salvation comes,
   The sound of rescued ones,
   And all this for a King.
   Angels join to sing, all for Christ, our King.

Offering

Words and Music by Paul Baloche

Strum Pattern: 4
Pick Pattern: 5

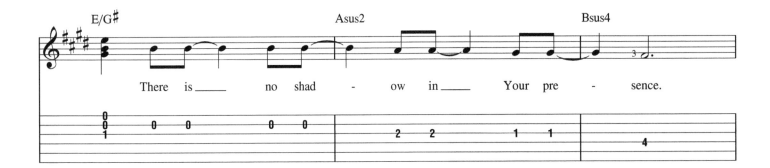

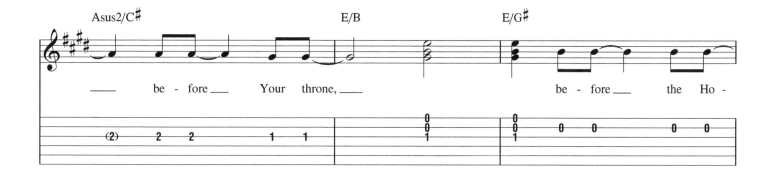

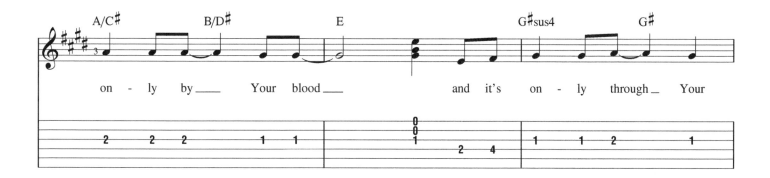

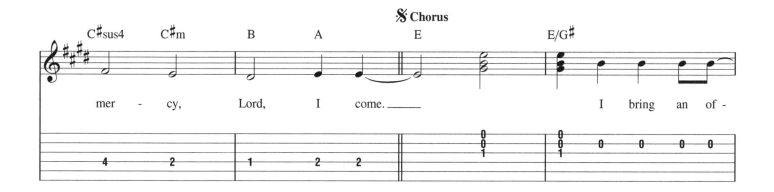

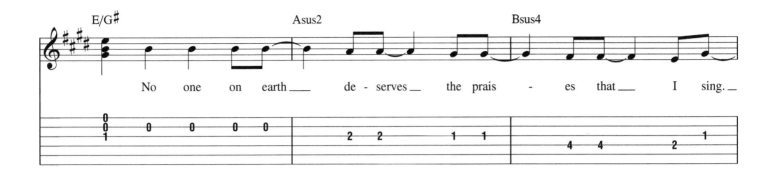

No one on earth __ de - serves __ the prais - es that __ I sing. __

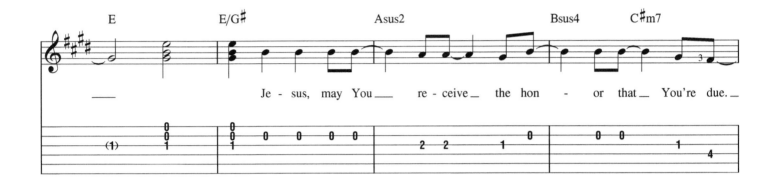

__ Je - sus, may You __ re - ceive __ the hon - or that __ You're due. __

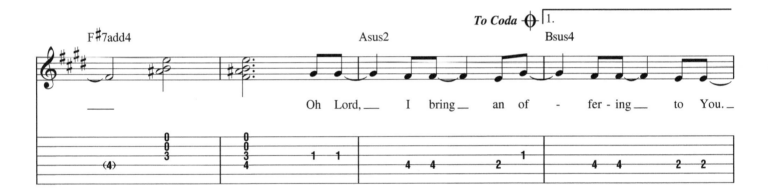

To Coda ⊕ 1.

Oh Lord, __ I bring __ an of - fer - ing __ to You. __

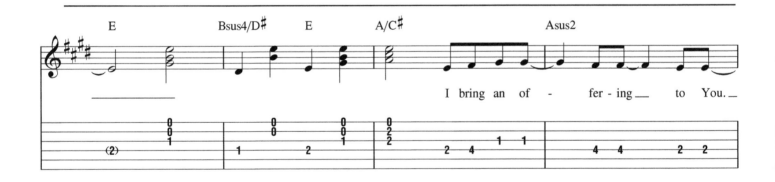

I bring an of - fer - ing __ to You. __

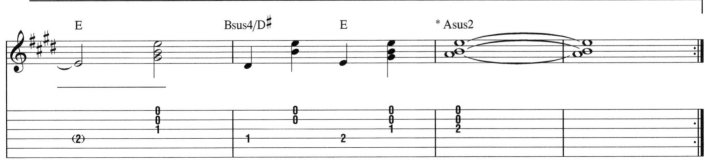

*Let chord ring.

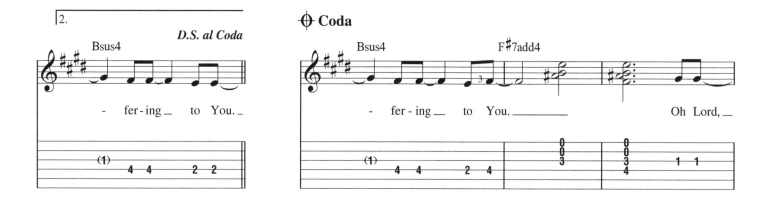

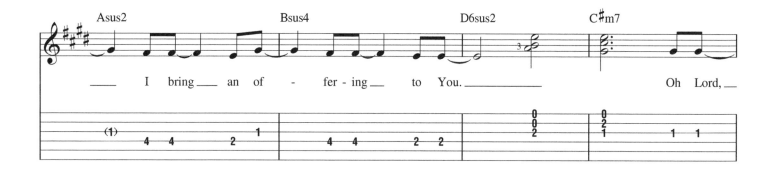

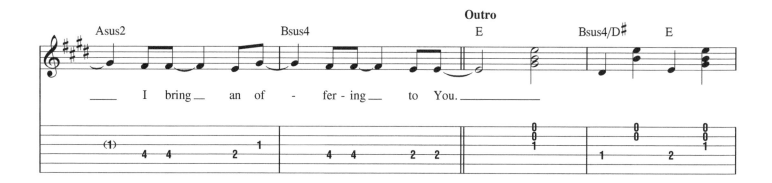

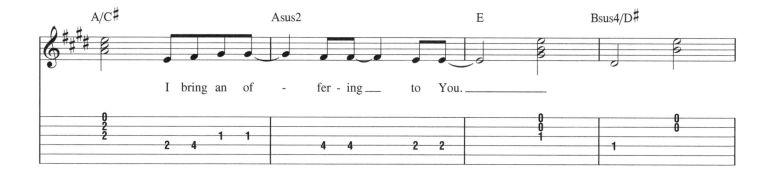

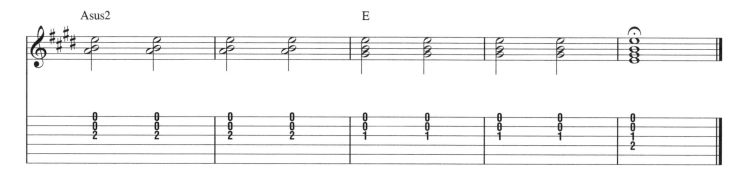

Our God Saves

Words and Music by Paul Baloche and Brenton Brown

Strum Pattern: 1, 2
Pick Pattern: 4, 5

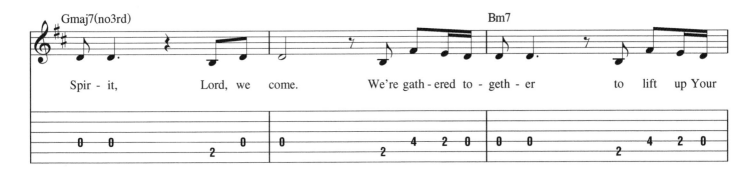

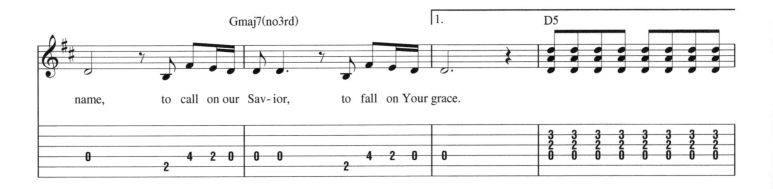

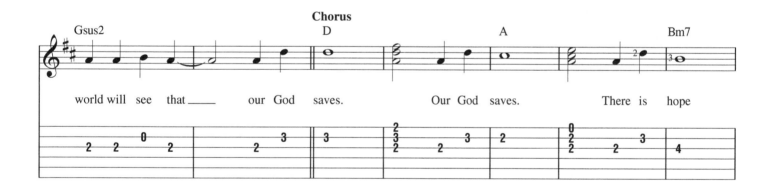

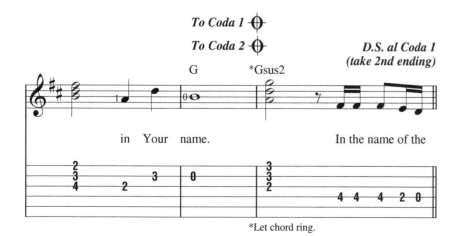

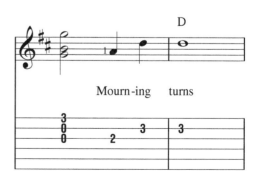

*Let chord ring.

to songs of praise Our God saves. our God saves. Yeah. ___

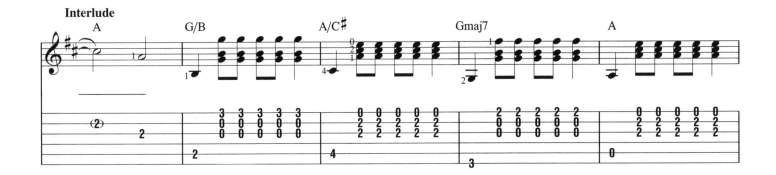

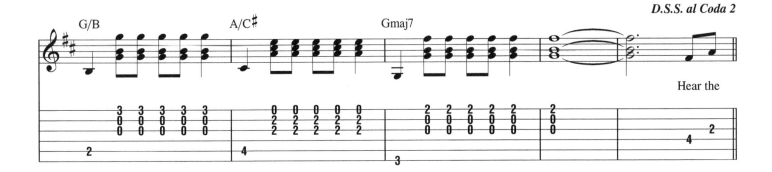

D.S.S. al Coda 2

Hear the

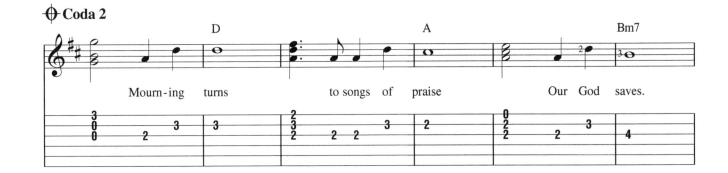

Mourn-ing turns to songs of praise Our God saves.

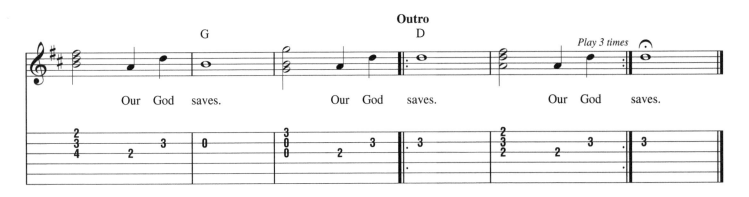

Our God saves. Our God saves. Our God saves.

The Potter's Hand

Words and Music by Darlene Zschech

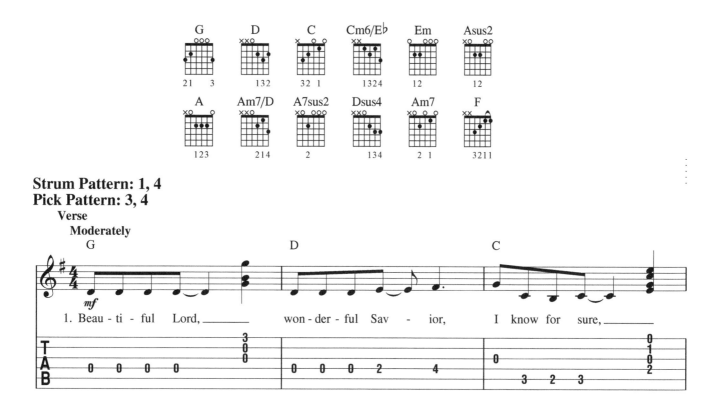

Strum Pattern: 1, 4
Pick Pattern: 3, 4

Verse
Moderately

1. Beau - ti - ful Lord, _____ won - der - ful Sav - ior, I know for sure, _____ all of my days _____ are held in Your hand, _____ craft - ed in - to _____ Your

per - fect plan. _____ 2., 3. You gen - tly call _____ me in - to Your pres - ence,

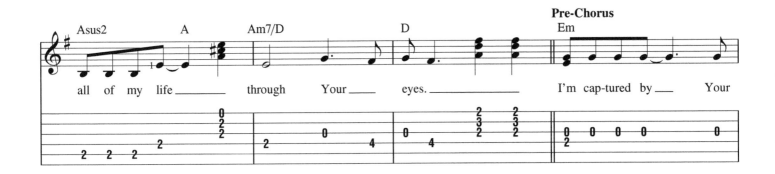

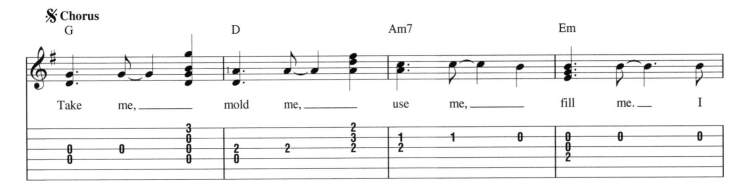

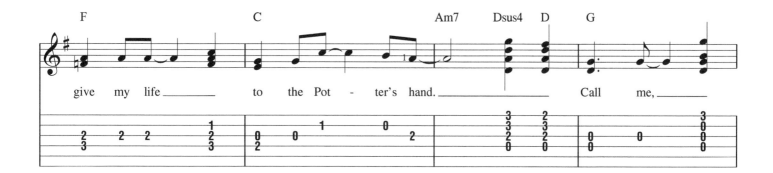

give my life _____ to the Pot - ter's hand. _____ Call me,

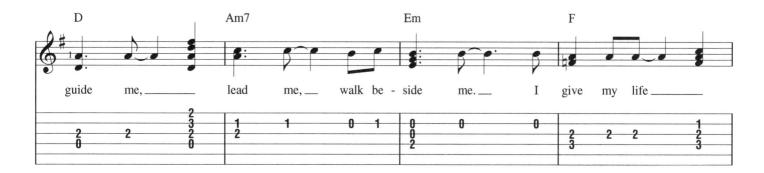

guide me, _____ lead me, ___ walk be - side me. ___ I give my life _____

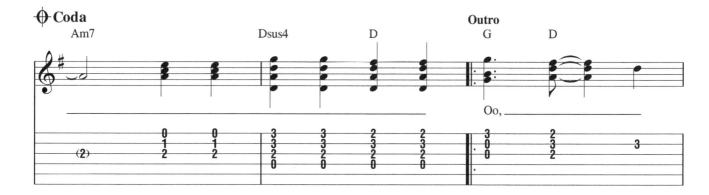

to the Pot - ter's hand. _____

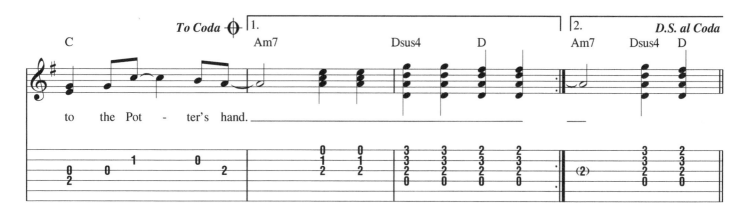

Oo, _____

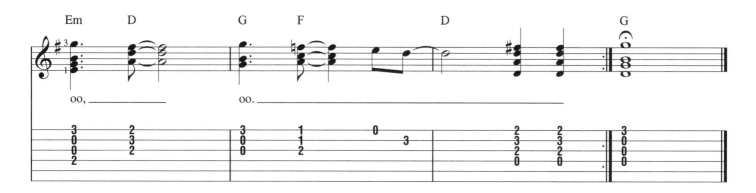

oo, _____ oo.

Revelation Song

Words and Music by Jennie Lee Riddle

Strum Pattern: 3
Pick Pattern: 4

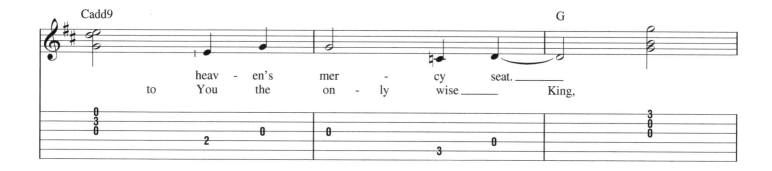

heav - en's mer - cy seat. ____

to You the on - ly wise ____ King,

Chorus

oh.

Ho - ly, ho - ly, ho - ly

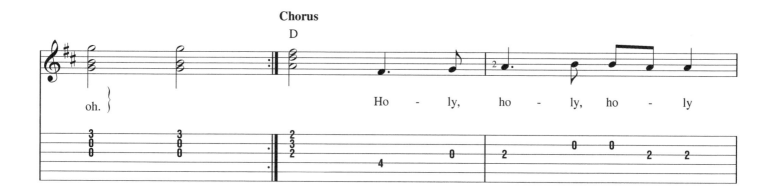

is the ____ Lord God Al - might - y, who was ____ and is ____

____ and is ____ to come. ____

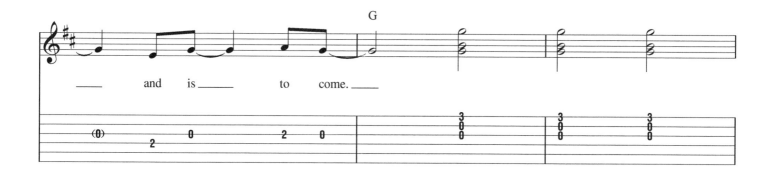

With all cre - a - tion I ____ sing praise to the

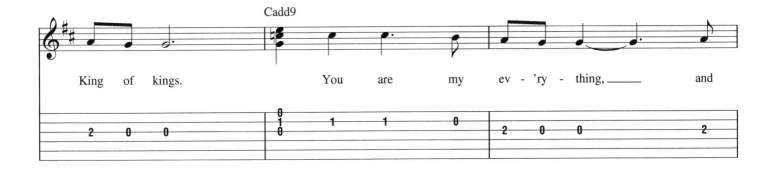

King of kings. You are my ev - 'ry - thing, _____ and

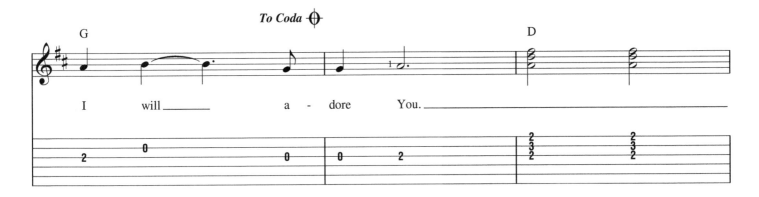

I will _____ a - dore You. _____

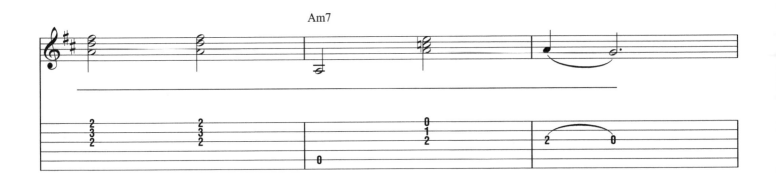

I _____ will _____ a - dore _____ You, _____

⊕ Coda

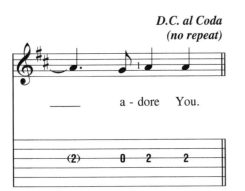

_____ a - dore You.

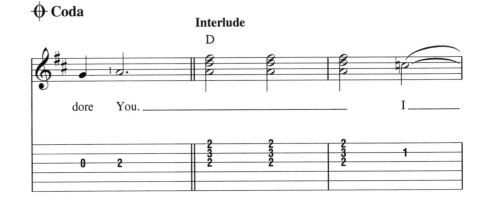

dore You. _____ I _____

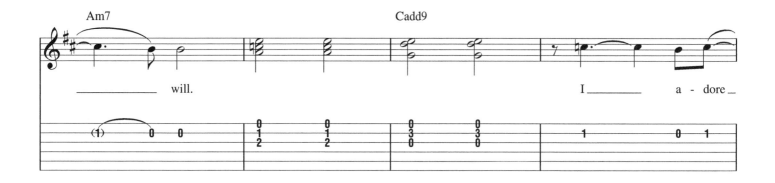

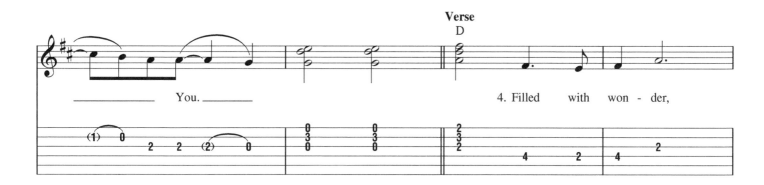

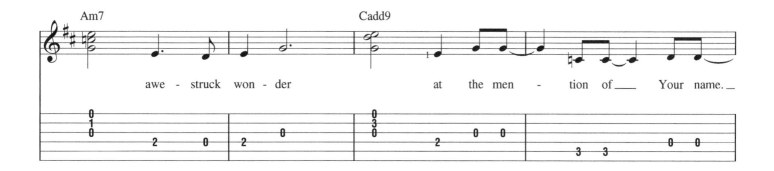

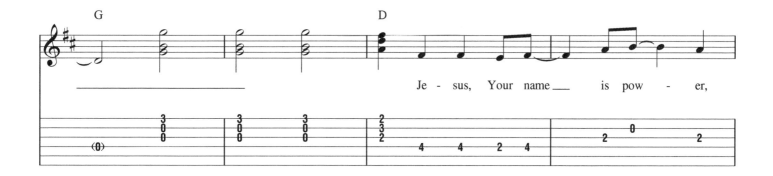

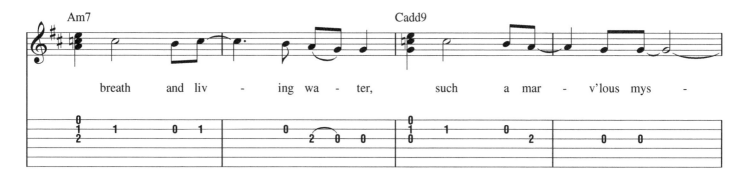

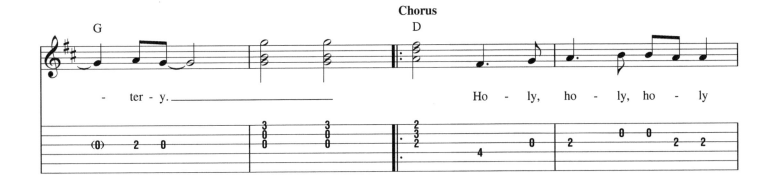

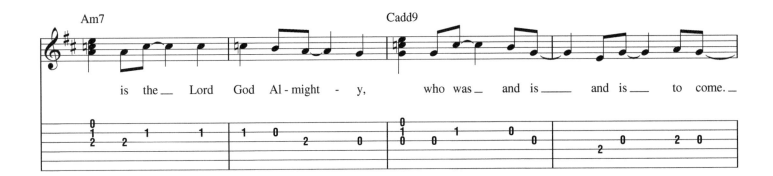

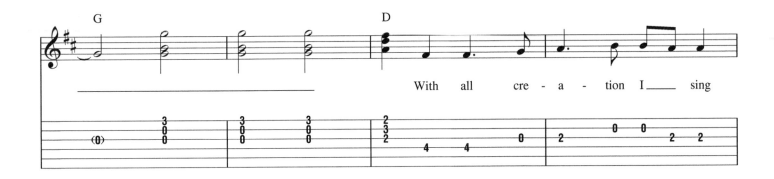

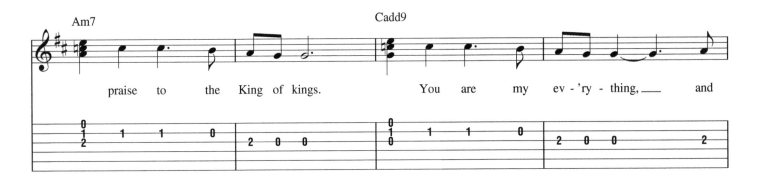

Sing to the King

Words and Music by Billy James Foote

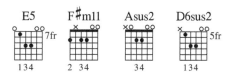

Strum Pattern: 1
Pick Pattern: 4

Intro
Moderately

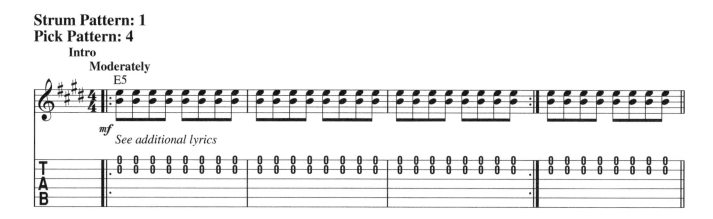

mf
See additional lyrics

Verse

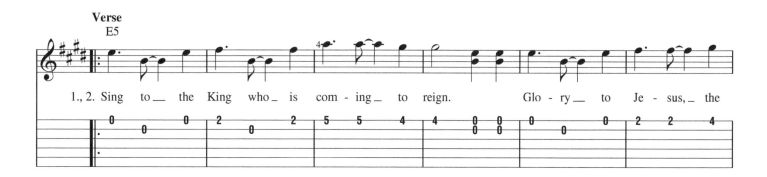

1., 2. Sing to __ the King who __ is com - ing __ to reign. Glo - ry __ to Je - sus, __ the

Lamb that __ was slain. Life and __ sal - va - tion __ His em - pire __ shall bring, and

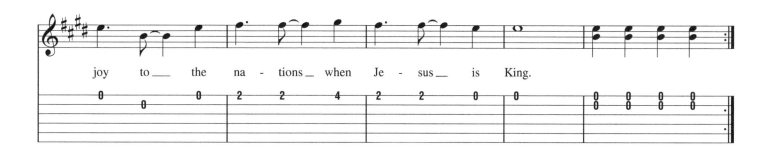

joy to __ the na - tions __ when Je - sus __ is King.

*Sung one octave higher throughout Chorus.

*Sung one octave higher till end.

Additional Lyrics

Intro Spoken: Let this declaration rise up across this field
That we are a chosen generation,
We are loved by God, and we belong to Him,
And He is ev'rything that we need.

Today Is the Day

Words and Music by Lincoln Brewster and Paul Baloche

Strum Pattern: 1
Pick Pattern: 1

*Sung one octave
lower throughout,
except where noted.

know-ing that all You have_ in store for me is good, is good. To-day is the day You_have

*Sung as written throughout Chorus.

made; I will re - joice and be glad_ in it. To-day is the day You_ have made; I will re -

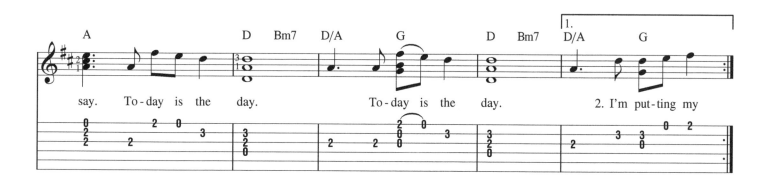

joice and be glad_ in it. And I won't wor - ry a - bout to - mor - row, I'm trust-ing in what_You

**3rd time, substitute D/A.

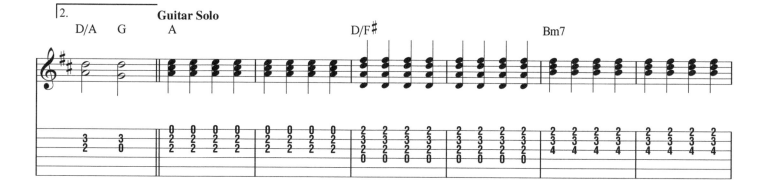

say. To - day is the day. To - day is the day. 2. I'm put-ting my

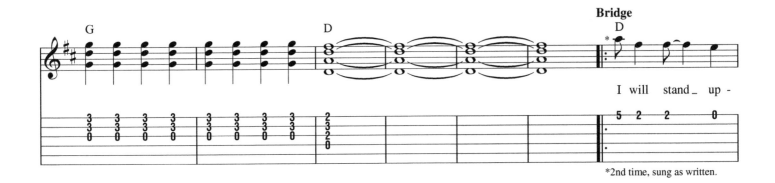

*2nd time, sung as written.

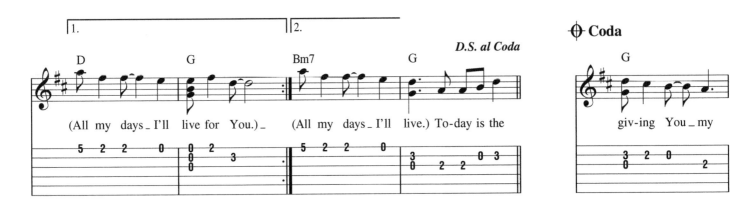

Worthy Is the Lamb

Words and Music by Darlene Zschech

Strum Pattern: 5
Pick Pattern: 1

Piano arr. for gtr., next 4 meas.

hands. Washed me in Your cleans-ing flow, _ now all I know, Your for - give - ness and _ em - brace.

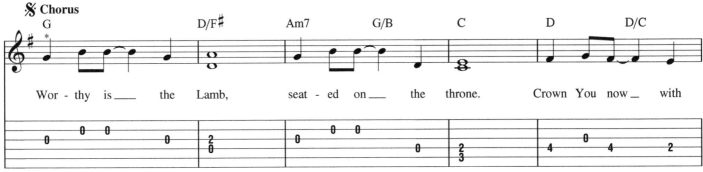

𝄋 Chorus

Wor - thy is ___ the Lamb, seat - ed on ___ the throne. Crown You now _ with

*Sung one octave higher throughout Chorus.

man - y crowns, _ You reign vic - to - ri - ous. High and lift - ed up,

Je - sus, Son _ of God. ___ The dar - ling of heav - en cru - ci - fied.

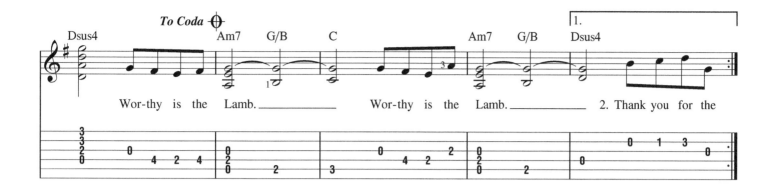

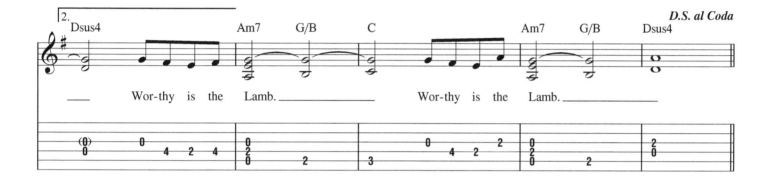

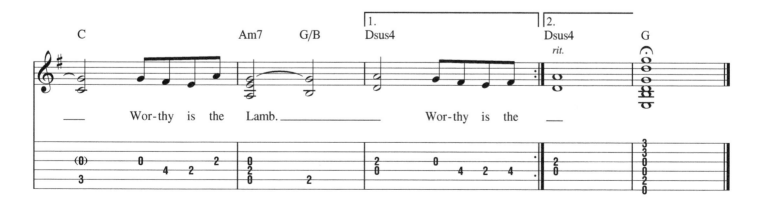

You Are My King
(Amazing Love)

Words and Music by Billy James Foote

Strum Pattern: 6
Pick Pattern: 4

Chorus

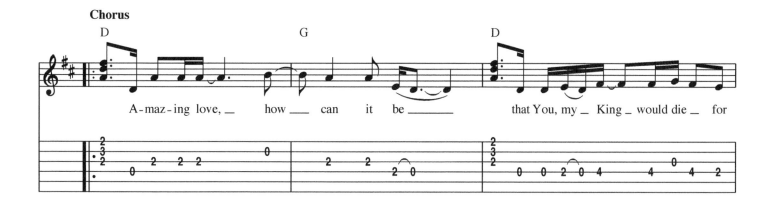

A-maz-ing love, __ how __ can it be _____ that You, my _ King _ would die _ for

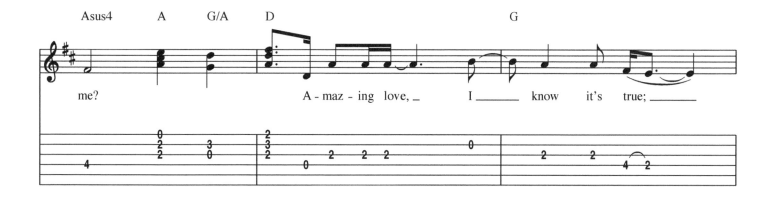

me? A-maz-ing love, _ I _____ know it's true; _____

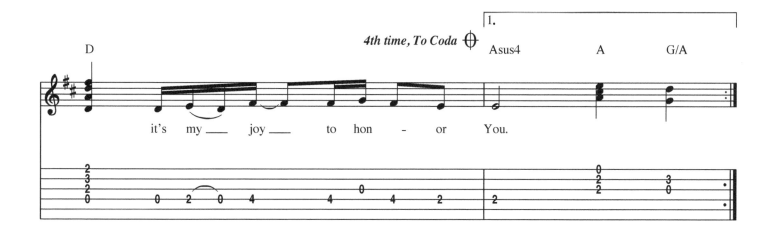

it's my ___ joy ___ to hon - or You.

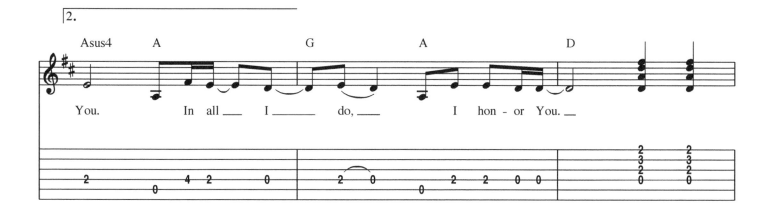

You. In all ___ I _____ do, ___ I hon - or You. __

Interlude

You _____ are _ my _____ King.

You _____ are _ my _____ King. Je - sus, You _____ are _ my _

D.S. al Coda
(take repeats)

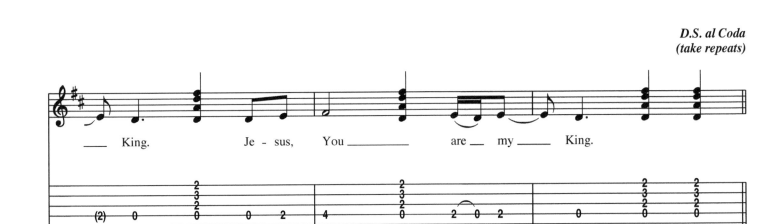

_ King. Je - sus, You _____ are _ my _____ King.

⊕ Coda

You. In all _ I _____ do, ___ I hon - or You. _

Your Grace Is Enough

Words and Music by Matt Maher

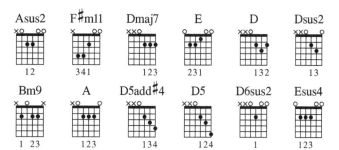

Strum Pattern: 1
Pick Pattern: 5

Intro
Joyfully

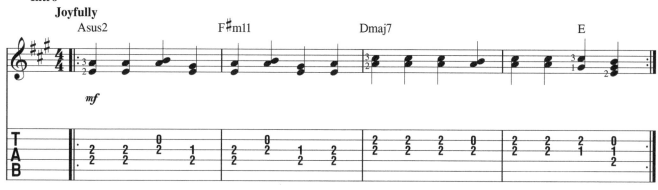

Verse

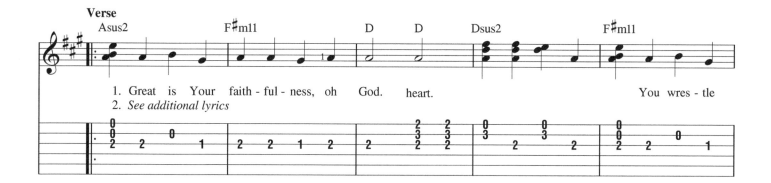

1. Great is Your faith-ful-ness, oh God. heart.
2. *See additional lyrics*

You wres-tle

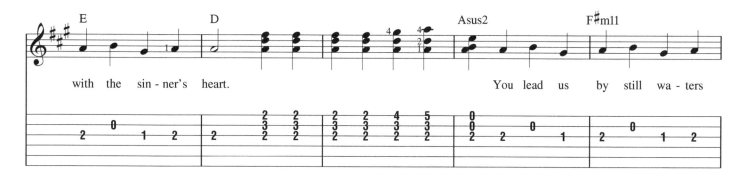

with the sin-ner's heart.   You lead us   by   still wa-ters

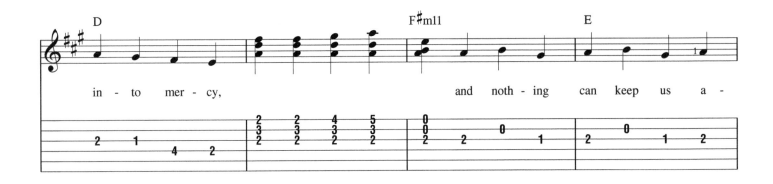

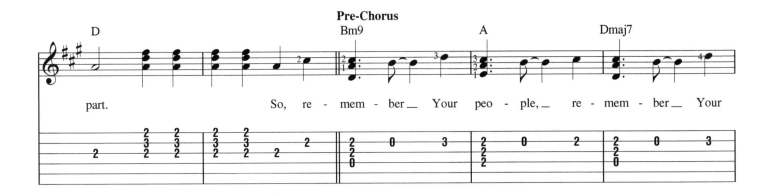

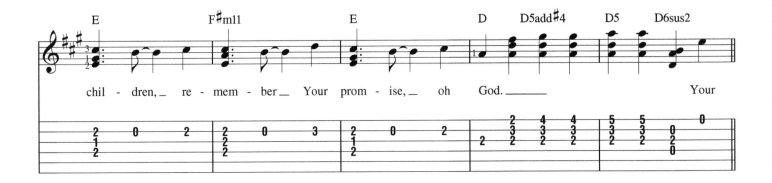

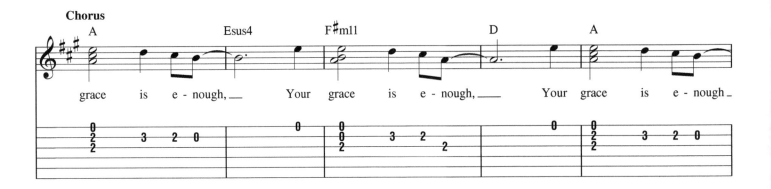

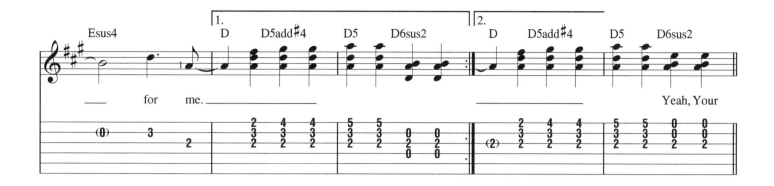

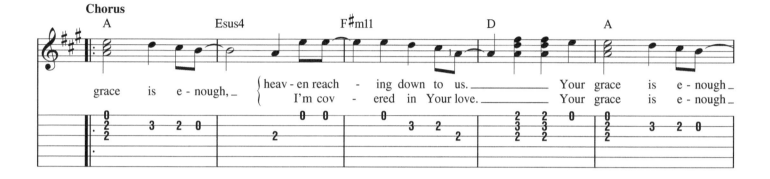

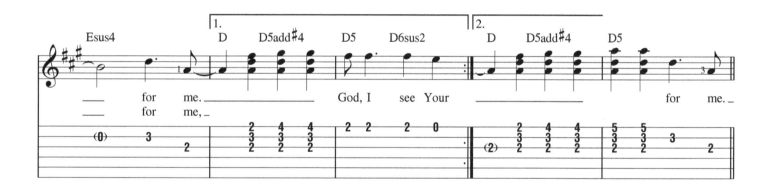

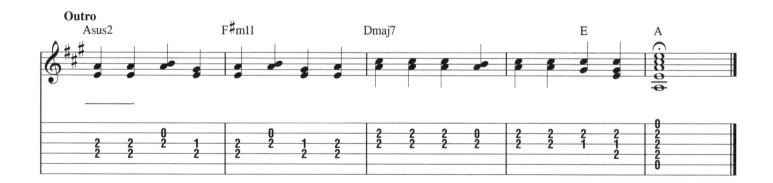

Additional Lyrics

2. Great is Your love and justice, God.
   You use the weak to lead the strong.
   You lead us in the song of Your salvation,
   And all Your people sing along.

You Never Let Go

Words and Music by Matt Redman and Beth Redman

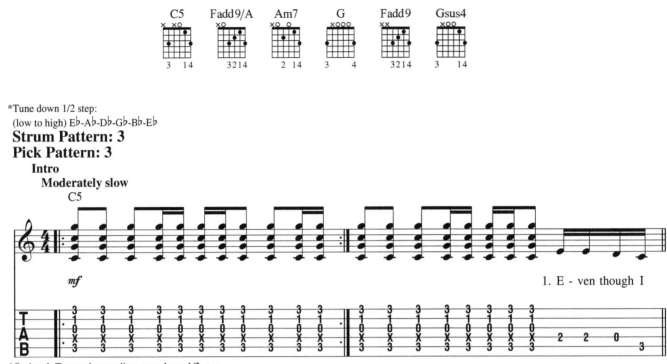

*Tune down 1/2 step:
(low to high) Eb-Ab-Db-Gb-Bb-Eb

Strum Pattern: 3
Pick Pattern: 3

Intro
Moderately slow

*Optional: To match recording, tune down 1/2 step.

walk __ through the val - ley of the sha - dow of death, __ Your per - fect love is cast - ing out fear. __
light __ that is com - ing for the heart that holds on, ___ a glo - rious light be - yond all com - pare. __

And e - ven when I'm caught __ in the mid - dle of the storms of this life, __ I
And there will be an end ___ to these trou - bles, but un - til that day comes, _ we'll

won't turn back; I know You are near. —
live to know You here on the earth. —
And I will fear no e - vil, for my God is

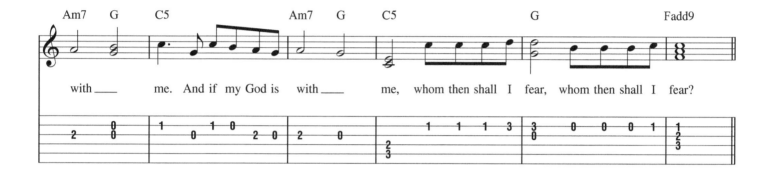

with ___ me. And if my God is with ___ me, whom then shall I fear, whom then shall I fear?

𝄋 Chorus

Oh, no, You nev-er let go, through the calm and through the storm. Oh, no, You nev-er let go, in

ev-'ry high and ev-'ry low. Oh, no, You nev-er let go, Lord, You nev-er let go of me. —

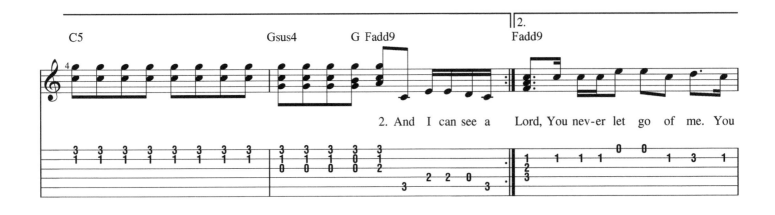

2. And I can see a Lord, You nev-er let go of me. You

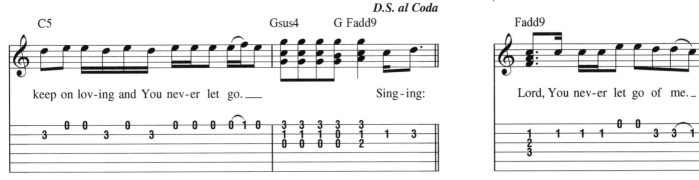

D.S. al Coda

Coda

keep on lov-ing and You nev-er let go. ___ Sing-ing:

Lord, You nev-er let go of me. ___

Bridge

Yes, I can see a light that is com-ing for the

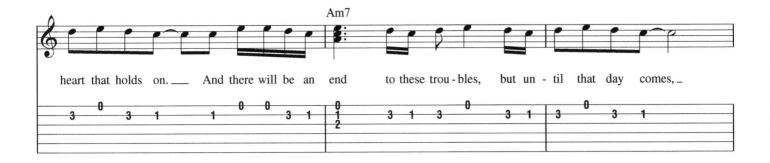

heart that holds on. ___ And there will be an end to these trou-bles, but un-til that day comes, ___

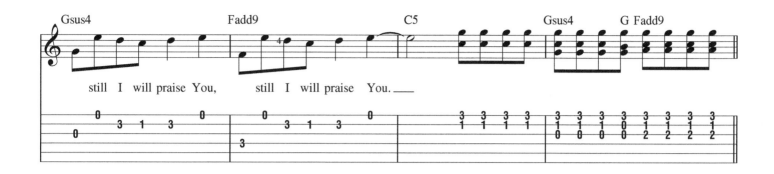

still I will praise You, still I will praise You. ___

Outro-Chorus

Oh, no, You nev-er let go, through the calm and through the storm. Oh, no, You nev-er let go, in

ev-'ry high and ev-'ry low. Oh, no, You nev-er let go, Lord, You nev-er let go of me.

Lord, you nev-er let go of me. ___ Lord, You nev-er let go of me. ___

This series features simplified arrangements with notes, tab, chord charts, and strum and pick patterns.

MIXED FOLIOS

00702287 Acoustic	$16.99
00702002 Acoustic Rock Hits for Easy Guitar	$15.99
00702166 All-Time Best Guitar Collection	$19.99
00702232 Best Acoustic Songs for Easy Guitar	$14.99
00119835 Best Children's Songs	$16.99
00702233 Best Hard Rock Songs	$15.99
00703055 The Big Book of Nursery Rhymes & Children's Songs	$16.99
00698978 Big Christmas Collection	$17.99
00702394 Bluegrass Songs for Easy Guitar	$12.99
00289632 Bohemian Rhapsody	$17.99
00703387 Celtic Classics	$14.99
00224808 Chart Hits of 2016-2017	$14.99
00267383 Chart Hits of 2017-2018	$14.99
00334293 Chart Hits of 2019-2020	$16.99
00702149 Children's Christian Songbook	$9.99
00702028 Christmas Classics	$8.99
00101779 Christmas Guitar	$14.99
00702185 Christmas Hits	$10.99
00702141 Classic Rock	$8.95
00159642 Classical Melodies	$12.99
00253933 Disney/Pixar's Coco	$16.99
00702203 CMT's 100 Greatest Country Songs	$29.99
00702283 The Contemporary Christian Collection	$16.99
00196954 Contemporary Disney	$19.99

00702239 Country Classics for Easy Guitar	$22.99
00702257 Easy Acoustic Guitar Songs	$14.99
00702280 Easy Guitar Tab White Pages	$29.99
00702041 Favorite Hymns for Easy Guitar	$10.99
00222701 Folk Pop Songs	$14.99
00126894 Frozen	$14.99
00333922 Frozen 2	$14.99
00702286 Glee	$16.99
00702160 The Great American Country Songbook	$16.99
00267383 Great American Gospel for Guitar	$12.99
00702050 Great Classical Themes for Easy Guitar	$8.99
00702116 Greatest Hymns for Guitar	$10.99
00275088 The Greatest Showman	$17.99
00148030 Halloween Guitar Songs	$14.99
00702273 Irish Songs	$12.99
00192503 Jazz Classics for Easy Guitar	$14.99
00702275 Jazz Favorites for Easy Guitar	$15.99
00702274 Jazz Standards for Easy Guitar	$17.99
00702162 Jumbo Easy Guitar Songbook	$19.99
00232285 La La Land	$16.99
00702258 Legends of Rock	$14.99
00702189 MTV's 100 Greatest Pop Songs	$24.95
00702272 1950s Rock	$15.99
00702271 1960s Rock	$15.99
00702270 1970s Rock	$16.99
00702269 1980s Rock	$15.99

00702268 1990s Rock	$19.99
00109725 Once	$14.99
00702187 Selections from O Brother Where Art Thou?	$19.99
00702178 100 Songs for Kids	$14.99
00702515 Pirates of the Caribbean	$16.99
00702125 Praise and Worship for Guitar	$10.99
00287930 Songs from *A Star Is Born, The Greatest Showman, La La Land,* and More Movie Musicals	$16.99
00702285 Southern Rock Hits	$12.99
00156420 Star Wars Music	$14.99
00121535 30 Easy Celtic Guitar Solos	$15.99
00702156 3-Chord Rock	$12.99
00702220 Today's Country Hits	$12.99
00244654 Top Hits of 2017	$14.99
00283786 Top Hits of 2018	$14.99
00702294 Top Worship Hits	$15.99
00702255 VH1's 100 Greatest Hard Rock Songs	$29.99
00702175 VH1's 100 Greatest Songs of Rock and Roll	$27.99
00702253 Wicked	$12.99

ARTIST COLLECTIONS

00702267 AC/DC for Easy Guitar	$15.99
00702598 Adele for Easy Guitar	$15.99
00156221 Adele – 25	$16.99
00702040 Best of the Allman Brothers	$16.99
00702865 J.S. Bach for Easy Guitar	$14.99
00702169 Best of The Beach Boys	$12.99
00702292 The Beatles — 1	$19.99
00125796 Best of Chuck Berry	$15.99
00702201 The Essential Black Sabbath	$12.95
00702250 blink-182 — Greatest Hits	$16.99
02501615 Zac Brown Band — The Foundation	$19.99
02501621 Zac Brown Band — You Get What You Give	$16.99
00702043 Best of Johnny Cash	$16.99
00702090 Eric Clapton's Best	$12.99
00702086 Eric Clapton — from the Album Unplugged	$15.99
00702202 The Essential Eric Clapton	$15.99
00702053 Best of Patsy Cline	$15.99
00222697 Very Best of Coldplay – 2nd Edition	$14.99
00702229 The Very Best of Creedence Clearwater Revival	$15.99
00702145 Best of Jim Croce	$15.99
00702219 David Crowder*Band Collection	$12.95
00702278 Crosby, Stills & Nash	$12.99
14042809 Bob Dylan	$14.99
00702276 Fleetwood Mac — Easy Guitar Collection	$16.99
00139462 The Very Best of Grateful Dead	$15.99
00702136 Best of Merle Haggard	$14.99
00702227 Jimi Hendrix — Smash Hits	$19.99
00702288 Best of Hillsong United	$12.99
00702236 Best of Antonio Carlos Jobim	$15.99

00702245 Elton John — Greatest Hits 1970–2002	$17.99
00129855 Jack Johnson	$16.99
00702204 Robert Johnson	$12.99
00702234 Selections from Toby Keith — 35 Biggest Hits	$12.95
00702003 Kiss	$16.99
00110578 Best of Kutless	$12.99
00702216 Lynyrd Skynyrd	$16.99
00702182 The Essential Bob Marley	$14.99
00146081 Maroon 5	$14.99
00121925 Bruno Mars – Unorthodox Jukebox	$12.99
00702248 Paul McCartney — All the Best	$14.99
00702129 Songs of Sarah McLachlan	$12.95
00125484 The Best of MercyMe	$12.99
02501316 Metallica — Death Magnetic	$19.99
00702209 Steve Miller Band — Young Hearts (Greatest Hits)	$12.95
00124167 Jason Mraz	$15.99
00702096 Best of Nirvana	$15.99
00702211 The Offspring — Greatest Hits	$12.95
00138026 One Direction	$14.99
00702030 Best of Roy Orbison	$16.99
00702144 Best of Ozzy Osbourne	$14.99
00702279 Tom Petty	$12.99
00102911 Pink Floyd	$16.99
00702139 Elvis Country Favorites	$17.99
00702293 The Very Best of Prince	$16.99
00699415 Best of Queen for Guitar	$15.99
00109279 Best of R.E.M.	$14.99
00702208 Red Hot Chili Peppers — Greatest Hits	$16.99
00198960 The Rolling Stones	$16.99
00174793 The Very Best of Santana	$14.99
00702196 Best of Bob Seger	$15.99

00146046 Ed Sheeran	$17.99
00702252 Frank Sinatra — Nothing But the Best	$17.99
00702010 Best of Rod Stewart	$16.99
00702049 Best of George Strait	$14.99
00702259 Taylor Swift for Easy Guitar	$15.99
00254499 Taylor Swift – Easy Guitar Anthology	$19.99
00702260 Taylor Swift — Fearless	$14.99
00139727 Taylor Swift — 1989	$17.99
00115960 Taylor Swift — Red	$16.99
00253667 Taylor Swift — Reputation	$17.99
00702290 Taylor Swift — Speak Now	$16.99
00702223 Chris Tomlin—Arriving	$16.99
00232849 Chris Tomlin Collection – 2nd Edition	$12.95
00702226 Chris Tomlin — See the Morning	$12.95
00148643 Train	$14.99
00702427 U2 — 18 Singles	$16.99
00702108 Best of Stevie Ray Vaughan	$16.99
00279005 The Who	$14.99
00702123 Best of Hank Williams	$15.99
00194548 Best of John Williams	$14.99
00702111 Stevie Wonder — Guitar Collection	$9.95
00702228 Neil Young — Greatest Hits	$15.99
00119133 Neil Young — Harvest	$14.99

Prices, contents and availability
subject to change without notice.

HAL•LEONARD®

Visit Hal Leonard online at **halleonard.com**

0720
306

christian guitar songbooks

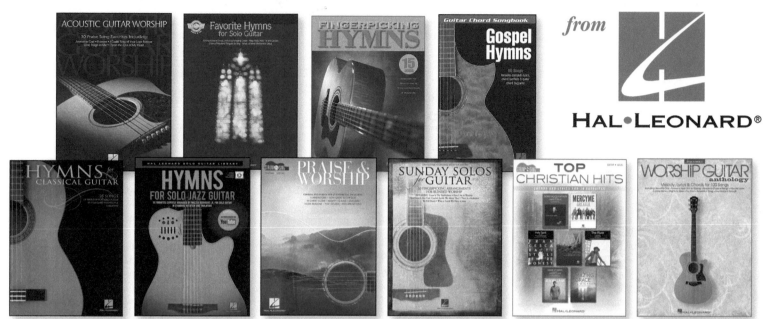

from

HAL•LEONARD®

ACOUSTIC GUITAR WORSHIP

30 praise song favorites arranged for guitar, including: Awesome God • Forever • I Could Sing of Your Love Forever • Lord, Reign in Me • Open the Eyes of My Heart • and more.

00699672 Solo Guitar $14.99

FAVORITE HYMNS FOR SOLO GUITAR

Amazing Grace • Christ the Lord Is Risen Today • For the Beauty of the Earth • Holy, Holy, Holy • In the Garden • Let Us Break Bread Together • O for a Thousand Tongues to Sing • Were You There? • What a Friend We Have in Jesus • When I Survey the Wondrous Cross • more.

00699275 Fingerstyle Guitar $12.99

FINGERPICKING HYMNS

Abide with Me • Amazing Grace • Beneath the Cross of Jesus • Come, Thou Fount of Every Blessing • For the Beauty of the Earth • A Mighty Fortress Is Our God • Rock of Ages • and more.

00699688 Solo Guitar $9.99

FINGERPICKING WORSHIP

Agnus Dei • Amazing Grace (My Chains Are Gone) • How Deep the Father's Love for Us • How Great Is Our God • I Worship You, Almighty God • More Precious Than Silver • There Is a Redeemer • We Fall Down • and more, plus an easy introduction to basic fingerstyle guitar.

00700554 Solo Guitar $10.99

GOSPEL GUITAR SONGBOOK

Includes notes & tab for fingerpicking and Travis picking arrangements of 15 favorites: Amazing Grace • Blessed Assurance • Do Lord • I've Got Peace Like a River • Just a Closer Walk with Thee • O Happy Day • Precious Memories • Rock of Ages • Swing Low, Sweet Chariot • There Is Power in the Blood • When the Saints Go Marching In • and more!

00695372 Guitar with Notes & Tab $9.95

GOSPEL HYMNS

Amazing Grace • At the Cross • Blessed Assurance • Higher Ground • I've Got Peace like a River • In the Garden • Love Lifted Me • The Old Rugged Cross • Rock of Ages • What a Friend We Have in Jesus • When the Saints Go Marching In • Wondrous Love • and more.

00700463
Lyrics/Chord Symbols/Guitar Chord Diagrams $14.99

HYMNS FOR CLASSICAL GUITAR

Amazing Grace • Be Thou My Vision • Come, Thou Fount of Every Blessing • For the Beauty of the Earth • Joyful, Joyful, We Adore Thee • My Faith Looks up to Thee • Rock of Ages • What a Friend We Have in Jesus • and more.

00701898 Solo Guitar $14.99

HYMNS FOR SOLO JAZZ GUITAR

Book/Online Video

Abide with Me • Amazing Grace • Blessed Assurance • God Is So Good • Just a Closer Walk with Thee • Londonderry Air • Oh How I Love Jesus • Softly and Tenderly • Sweet Hour of Prayer • What a Friend We Have in Jesus.

00153842 Solo Guitar $19.99

MODERN WORSHIP – GUITAR CHORD SONGBOOK

Amazed • Amazing Grace (My Chains Are Gone) • At the Cross • Beautiful One • Everlasting God • How Can I Keep from Singing • I Am Free • Let God Arise • Let My Words Be Few (I'll Stand in Awe of You) • Made to Worship • Mighty to Save • Nothing but the Blood • Offering • Sing to the King • Today Is the Day • Your Name • and more.

00701801
Lyrics/Chord Symbols/Guitar Chord Diagrams $16.99

PRAISE & WORSHIP – STRUM & SING

This inspirational collection features 25 favorites for guitarists to strum and sing. Includes chords and lyrics for: Amazing Grace (My Chains Are Gone) • Cornerstone • Everlasting God • Forever • The Heart of Worship • How Great Is Our God • In Christ Alone • Mighty to Save • 10,000 Reasons (Bless the Lord) • This I Believe • We Fall Down • and more.

00152381 Guitar/Vocal $12.99

SACRED SONGS FOR CLASSICAL GUITAR

Bind Us Together • El Shaddai • Here I Am, Lord • His Name Is Wonderful • How Great Thou Art • I Walked Today Where Jesus Walked • On Eagle's Wings • Thou Art Worthy • and more.

00702426 Guitar $14.99

SUNDAY SOLOS FOR GUITAR

Great Is Thy Faithfulness • Here I Am to Worship • How Great Is Our God • Joyful, Joyful, We Adore Thee • There Is a Redeemer • We Fall Down • What a Friend We Have in Jesus • and more!

00703083 Guitar $14.99

TOP CHRISTIAN HITS – STRUM & SING GUITAR

Good Good Father (Chris Tomlin) • Greater (MercyMe) • Holy Spirit (Francesca Battistelli) • I Am (Crowder) • Same Power (Jeremy Camp) • This Is Amazing Grace (Phil Wickham) • and more.

00156331 Guitar/Vocal $12.99

THE WORSHIP GUITAR ANTHOLOGY – VOLUME 1

This collection contains melody, lyrics & chords for 100 contemporary favorites, such as: Beautiful One • Forever • Here I Am to Worship • Hosanna (Praise Is Rising) • How He Loves • In Christ Alone • Mighty to Save • Our God • Revelation Song • Your Grace Is Enough • and dozens more.

00101864 Melody/Lyrics/Chords $16.99

WORSHIP SOLOS FOR FINGERSTYLE GUITAR

Ancient Words • Before the Throne of God Above • Broken Vessels (Amazing Grace) • Cornerstone • Good Good Father • Great Are You Lord • Holy Spirit • I Will Rise • King of My Heart • Lord, I Need You • O Come to the Altar • O Praise the Name (Anastasis) • Oceans (Where Feet May Fail) • 10,000 Reasons (Bless the Lord) • Your Name.

00276831 Guitar $14.99

TOP WORSHIP SONGS FOR GUITAR

Amazing Grace (My Chains Are Gone) • Because He Lives, Amen • Cornerstone • Forever (We Sing Hallelujah) • Good Good Father • Holy Spirit • Jesus Messiah • Lead Me to the Cross • Our God • Revelation Song • This Is Amazing Grace • We Believe • Your Grace Is Enough • and more.

00160854 Melody/Lyrics/Chords $12.99

Prices, contents and availability subject to change without notice.

**FOR MORE INFORMATION,
SEE YOUR LOCAL MUSIC DEALER,
OR WRITE TO:**

HAL•LEONARD®

7777 W. BLUEMOUND RD. P.O. BOX 13819
MILWAUKEE, WISCONSIN 53213

www.halleonard.com

Get Better at Guitar

...with these Great Guitar Instruction Books from Hal Leonard!

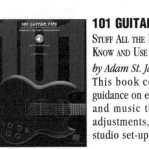

101 GUITAR TIPS
INCLUDES TAB
STUFF ALL THE PROS
KNOW AND USE
by Adam St. James
This book contains invaluable guidance on everything from scales and music theory to truss rod adjustments, proper recording studio set-ups, and much more.
00695737 Book/Online Audio $16.99

AMAZING PHRASING
INCLUDES TAB
by Tom Kolb
This book/audio pack explores all the main components necessary for crafting well-balanced rhythmic and melodic phrases. It also explains how these phrases are put together to form cohesive solos. The companion audio contains 89 demo tracks, most with full-band backing.
00695583 Book/Online Audio $19.99

ARPEGGIOS FOR THE MODERN GUITARIST
INCLUDES TAB
by Tom Kolb
Using this no-nonsense book with online audio, guitarists will learn to apply and execute all types of arpeggio forms using a variety of techniques, including alternate picking, sweep picking, tapping, string skipping, and legato.
00695862 Book/Online Audio $19.99

BLUES YOU CAN USE
by John Ganapes
This comprehensive source for learning blues guitar is designed to develop both your lead and rhythm playing. Includes: 21 complete solos • blues chords, progressions and riffs • turnarounds • movable scales and soloing techniques • string bending • utilizing the entire fingerboard • and more.
00142420 Book/Online Media.................$19.99

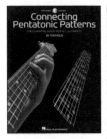

CONNECTING PENTATONIC PATTERNS
INCLUDES TAB
by Tom Kolb
If you've been finding yourself trapped in the pentatonic box, this book is for you! This hands-on book with online audio offers examples for guitar players of all levels, from beginner to advanced. Study this book faithfully, and soon you'll be soloing all over the neck with the greatest of ease.
00696445 Book/Online Audio $19.99

FRETBOARD MASTERY
INCLUDES TAB
by Troy Stetina
Untangle the mysterious regions of the guitar fretboard and unlock your potential. This book familiarizes you with all the shapes you need to know by applying them in real musical examples, thereby reinforcing and reaffirming your newfound knowledge.
00695331 Book/Online Audio $19.99

GUITAR AEROBICS
INCLUDES TAB
by Troy Nelson
Here is a daily dose of guitar "vitamins" to keep your chops fine tuned! Musical styles include rock, blues, jazz, metal, country, and funk. Techniques taught include alternate picking, arpeggios, sweep picking, string skipping, legato, string bending, and rhythm guitar.
00695946 Book/Online Audio $19.99

GUITAR CLUES
INCLUDES TAB
OPERATION PENTATONIC
by Greg Koch
Whether you're new to improvising or have been doing it for a while, this book/audio pack will provide loads of delicious licks and tricks that you can use right away, from volume swells and chicken pickin' to intervallic and chordal ideas.
00695827 Book/Online Audio $19.99

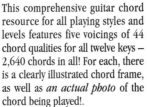

PAT METHENY – GUITAR ETUDES
INCLUDES TAB
Over the years, in many master classes and workshops around the world, Pat has demonstrated the kind of daily workout he puts himself through. This book includes a collection of 14 guitar etudes he created to help you limber up, improve picking technique and build finger independence.
00696587...$15.99

PICTURE CHORD ENCYCLOPEDIA
This comprehensive guitar chord resource for all playing styles and levels features five voicings of 44 chord qualities for all twelve keys – 2,640 chords in all! For each, there is a clearly illustrated chord frame, as well as *an actual photo* of the chord being played!.
00695224...$19.99

RHYTHM GUITAR 365
INCLUDES TAB
by Troy Nelson
This book provides 365 exercises – one for every day of the year! – to keep your rhythm chops fine tuned. Topics covered include: chord theory; the fundamentals of rhythm; fingerpicking; strum patterns; diatonic and non-diatonic progressions; triads; major and minor keys; and more.
00103627 Book/Online Audio $24.99

SCALE CHORD RELATIONSHIPS
INCLUDES TAB
by Michael Mueller & Jeff Schroedl
This book/audio pack explains how to: recognize keys • analyze chord progressions • use the modes • play over nondiatonic harmony • use harmonic and melodic minor scales • use symmetrical scales • incorporate exotic scales • and much more!
00695563 Book/Online Audio $14.99

SPEED MECHANICS FOR LEAD GUITAR
INCLUDES TAB
by Troy Stetina
Take your playing to the stratosphere with this advanced lead book which will help you develop speed and precision in today's explosive playing styles. Learn the fastest ways to achieve speed and control, secrets to make your practice time really count, and how to open your ears and make your musical ideas more solid and tangible.
00699323 Book/Online Audio $19.99

TOTAL ROCK GUITAR
INCLUDES TAB
by Troy Stetina
This comprehensive source for learning rock guitar is designed to develop both lead and rhythm playing. It covers: getting a tone that rocks • open chords, power chords and barre chords • riffs, scales and licks • string bending, strumming, and harmonics • and more.
00695246 Book/Online Audio $19.99

Guitar World Presents STEVE VAI'S GUITAR WORKOUT
INCLUDES TAB
In this book, Steve Vai reveals his path to virtuoso enlightenment with two challenging guitar workouts – one 10-hour and one 30-hour – which include scale and chord exercises, ear training, sight-reading, music theory, and much more.
00119643...$14.99

HAL•LEONARD®